The Investor's

Self-Teaching Seminars

INVESTING IN RENTAL PROPERTIES

The Investor's
Self-Teaching Seminars

INVESTING IN RENTAL PROPERTIES

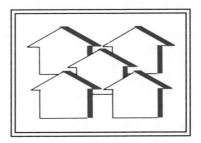

One of a Series of Hands-On Workshops
Dedicated to the Serious Investor

Robert W. Richards
Grover C. Richards

Probus Publishing Company
Chicago, Illinois

ISBN 0-917253-76-0

Printed in the United States of America

3 4 5 6 7 8 9 0

Preface

This book reveals the essentials of the real estate business in a perspective geared toward existing and potential investors of single-family homes, duplexes, triplexes, and so on. It covers such major topics as real estate business cycles, advantages and disadvantages, investment planning and strategy development, evaluating risk, getting started, selecting/avoiding properties, negotiating, pertinent contractual terminology, cash flow analysis, internal rate of return, income tax aspects, contemporary financing techniques, and selling. The approach taken to these areas is "hands-on" in that problem-solving situations (generally involving financial analysis), and investor's purchasing checklist, and real-life examples are presented.

In light of current changes within the real estate industry—more specifically, tax legislation—single-family rental homes appear to be in the best position for investment. Large rental properties, on the other hand, are not expected to fare particularly well for investors because of significant changes in the way real estate projects and the holding of limited partnership interests are taxed. In the past, raising money for these projects, especially large apartment complexes, was relatively easy because of the preferred tax treatment of real estate and limited partnership interests. Today, however, raising money for large apartment developments will not be as easy, nor is their economic attractiveness as evident; therefore, fewer of them will be built.

In contrast, the appeal of investing in *single-family homes* by an ''active participant'' is tremendous because of the more favorable tax treatment provided for these participants and the ability to sell in a bigger, faster-paced market. Because fewer apartments are to be built, rents are expected to steadily rise, which will help keep single-family homes rented at a fair monthly rental. In addition, when the time comes to sell, a single-family home can be put on the residential real estate market, which is ordinarily much more vigorous and continuous than the commercial real estate markets. Moreover, the latter is more heavily influenced by tax law changes than the former.

Investors of securities, commodities, and collectibles can enjoy the diversity and some tax benefits offered by investing in residential property. This book is written for investors, especially those who are not familiar with the real estate industry. After acquiring the appropriate knowledge, however, any investor can profit from real property ownership. Huge fortunes have been made by using some creativity, developing certain skills, taking on selected risks, and following through.

There are exactly two ways of approaching an investment venture: (1) with some skill and knowledge or (2) without any skill or knowledge. Obviously, the first approach is better. If you do not have skill or knowledge in real estate investing then you must obtain it through study and experience or through experience alone. Study and experience is the preferred course, however, because experience alone usually requires a longer period of time and can become prohibitively expensive.

We would like to thank the following people for their generous help in the preparation of this book: Charles Leonard, Milly Richards, Woody Dickerson, Jon Volz, Gary Brock, Bill Droms, Chet Richards, and the people at Probus Publishing Company.

Robert W. Richards
Grover C. Richards

CONTENTS

Prologue

_____

_____

_____

AN OVERVIEW

This chapter will present the basics of real estate investing. All real estate investors must be aware of what real property consists of, its investment environment, factors causing changes in value, and the advantages and disadvantages of these investments.

REAL PROPERTY VERSUS PERSONAL PROPERTY

Real estate (and generally realty or real property) is land, all improvements intended to be affixed to land in a permanent manner, and the rights to use them. Land begins at the earth's center (subsurface rights) and continues through the earth's surface (surface rights) and into space (air rights). Improvements are constructive or useful changes made to land, such as buildings, roads, fences, landscaping, sewer lines, electric lines, grading, and drainage systems. Some of the more common rights associated with land ownership include the right to build, occupy, use, lease, sell, extract natural resources, farm, grant easements, mortgage, exclude others, abandon, gift, devise (will to others), and covenant (promise in the conveyance of real estate).

Personal property (personalty), on the other hand, refers to all movable property that is not permanently affixed to land (i.e., anything not classified as real estate). Examples include automobiles, boats, furniture, clothes, books, stock certificates, bonds, and jewelry. Note that personal property can also become real property, depending on where it winds up. For example, plumbing fixtures, wire, lumber, bricks, nails, cement, and paint purchased from a building supply store are personal property until they are permanently placed in a structure, at which point they become real property.

THE INVESTMENT ENVIRONMENT

Investing in real estate is quite different from investing in many other assets: there is no organized exchange on which real estate transactions are made; no two properties are alike (heterogeneous assets); participants are not bound by a universally accepted set of ethical standards as are, for example, members of a stock exchange; transactions are conducted over an extended period of time; obtaining information (if it is available at all) is time-consuming; and there is a high degree of government involvement in the form of zoning ordinances, provisions covering county sewer lines, easements, taxes, eminent domain, etc. Many extraneous factors also have a direct influence on real estate transactions. These include interest rates, local business cycles, inflation cycles, urban land-use cycles, cultural changes, current popularity trends, and the threat of changes in tax laws. Purchasing real estate also requires a title search, title insurance, preparing and recording the deed, a survey, and other services—especially if money is borrowed to purchase it. To the informed investor, however, such an imperfect market can become quite profitable if he or she simply knows when to buy, hold, and sell.

There are different types of real estate investors. Most seasoned veterans specialize in a certain type of property in that they only deal in one particular area, such as strip shopping centers, subdividing undeveloped land, apartment complexes, industrial buildings, and office buildings. Usually the players in each category know each other, and many of the transactions of a specific type occur among the members of one of these groups. Investors who do not consider themselves to be sophisticated concerning real estate will probably

experience the greatest success dealing with small residential properties, particularly single-family homes along with duplexes, triplexes,
and quadraplexes. This is because (1) the market for such properties, especially single-family residences, is large (2) there is more
liquidity in small residential properties, especially single-family
homes, and (3) the market is not as sophisticated as it is in other
specialized areas (e.g., apartment buildings and office buildings).

FACTORS AFFECTING VALUE

DEMAND The most significant factor affecting real estate values
is demand. Demand refers to the degree to which ready, willing,
and able purchasers are going to buy a particular piece of real estate.
High *market demand* generally means that a large number of potential buyers exists, and, therefore the eventual selling price is expected
to be at or above appraised value.

But demand is not solely dependent on the number of potential
purchasers in that just one buyer and one seller are needed to make
a transaction. For example, you purchased 500 acres of Florida
swamp land for $20 an acre, and 10 years later (when its appraised
value is $50 an acre) a wealthy businessman comes along and wants
to buy your property right now. He offers you $100 an acre! You
do not want to sell, so you turn him down and then he counters
with an offer of $125 an acre. This buyer shows great willingness
to complete the transaction; in other words, individual demand is
high. What's the value of the swamp land? For the duration of the
second offer, it is $125 an acre, but when the offer expires and the
businessman decides to move on to something else, the value rapidly
diminishes. If there are no other prospective purchasers, the value
of your swamp land becomes zero—until a bona fide buyer can be
found—even through it has an appraised value of $50 an acre.
Individual demand, then, is the degree of willingness of *one* able
buyer to purchase a property.

From an investment standpoint, market demand is the principal
focus because individual demand, as a general rule, is neither as
predictable nor as stable. The number of expected bona fide future
purchasers is fundamentally important to an investor when deciding to acquire a certain property.

REAL ESTATE CYCLES   Like most other recurring events in the business world, demand tends to fluctuate in a cyclical manner. Although the demand cycle for real estate has high points and low points, it still has an overall tendency to slope up. In other words, real estate prices tend to increase over an extended period of time. Within the demand cycle are various subcycles that affect values (i.e., they are significant influences on or components of demand) of particular pieces of property at any given point in time. Unquestionably, the most notable subcycle is the inflation cycle.

Demand is affected by many factors. Some of the more common include personal tastes and attitudes of prospective buyers, level of technological change, sociological change, political climate, and availability of money. All such factors must be considered at a certain point in time. Each factor tends to fluctuate and usually results in an overall increase to the value of real property. For example, not long ago popular items included modern contemporary styles, energy efficient appliances, high-rise condominiums, fast write-off techniques for tax purposes, and imaginative financing arrangements. But different items may be popular tomorrow as styles and external influences (e.g., inflation, an energy crunch, a tight money market, and/or tax laws) change.

Most of the important factors (subcycles) affecting demand also seem to be cyclical. The subcycles include inflation, the local economy, popularity trends, construction, and interest rates. Although each one is different, they all have significant effects on the values of real property.

Inflation is, perhaps, the most important subcycle with regard to overall land prices. As inflation rises, real estate prices also rise, but usually at a faster rate. Because of monetary policies exercised by the Federal Reserve Board, however, interest rates tend to rise when inflation flares up, which can have a negative effect on real estate investment. As inflation slows down, on the other hand, a tight monetary policy is abolished (i.e., interest rates decline)—which generally allows inflation to return. Thus, the cycle continues.

Increases and decreases in aggregate prices, though, do not automatically affect all existing properties in every area at the same rate. Economic conditions at the local level also have a tremendous effect with the result that some areas may move counter to a trend. For example, in 1985 there was significant stagnation or decline in property values in Houston while the rest of the country experienced an increase in values. But when oil prices were high (1980), Houston had a higher rate of real-property price increases. Why did this happen? Any rise in price occurs when purchasers enter a market with the wherewithal for the properties they buy. When oil prices were high, production increased, more jobs became available, and, in effect, property values were bid up. The opposite occurred when oil prices dropped.

Another subcycle involves real estate transactions themselves. This is one area all real estate professionals and investors are painfully aware of because of the feast or famine nature of the business. The number of real estate transactions exercised during any one period is influenced by many factors, two of which are the local economy and interest rates. Perhaps the most important aspect of this subcycle is the *overkill phenomenon*. It occurs when pent-up demand is unleashed on a market in which not enough suitable properties are available. Developers rush to speculate as fast as they can in this market, purchasing and building properties at a stepped-up rate to meet the demand. However, these speculators are unable to predict the precise point at which the demand will be satisified. There is a time lag (say 2 to 24 months) between the point when developers recognize that the current market continues to be good and when construction is finally completed. As a result, many projects will not be completed before demand has dropped off. This will tend to bring real estate prices down—in a hurry. It is not unusual for this to happen in an area of the country that experiences rapid expansion or when a new concept is well received.

The popularity subcycle is another overkill phenomenon, but this one occurs among investors. It is usually stimulated by brokerage houses or news media or both. Outside investors are attracted to a certain type of property, a particular location, or a specific area where investors have already been successful. After a period of time, the market becomes glutted, prices fall, and the investment becomes unpopular. A new cycle begins when a different type of property becomes popular. Real estate investment trusts (REITs) and real estate limited partnerships are two examples. (Changes in investor's tax strategies also contribute to changes in the popularity cycle.)

The building cycle is closely tied to interest rates and the overkill phenomenon. When interest rates drop, contractors build to take advantage of pent-up demand for structures and the lower cost of borrowing. As stated earlier, builders, under normal conditions, will overproduce, leaving too many structures in a declining market. During the period of overproduction, however, prices have usually already peaked and interest rates will normally rise. A higher level of interest rates tend to constrain productivity until the rates fall again—yet another influential cycle.

Cyclical changes in interest rates have a pervasive effect on the value of real property. Along with the Federal Reserve, the investment community also influences interest rates through the money market. With a tight monetary control policy dictated by the Federal Reserve—when the rate of inflation is high or is expected to rise significantly—fewer buyers are able to enter the real estate market because they have to provide more equity to compensate for lower loan-to-value ratios or make higher mortgage payments. Obviously, prices will fall or stagnate. But when interest rates decline, prices tend to rise because more buyers have cash.

ADVANTAGES

As with any investment, you must continually weigh the advantages and disadvantages of a real estate transaction. Below are some of the advantages of investing in the real estate market, other than getting rich quick—which rarely happens. After thinking up some that fit your particular situation, review the ones we came up with and feel free to add any to your list.

1. Relatively stable values. Since about 1975 real estate prices have gone up steadily with only a few minor dips. Although cyclical, real property values do not typically fluctuate as rapidly as those of other investments. For example, under normal conditions, the price of a house one year ago will probably be fairly close to its value today, perhaps a little higher. Commodities, stocks, and bonds, on the other hand, are generally more likely to experience short-term fluctuations in value.

2. Immediate income. Investing in rental property can provide immediate cash flow, which can pay the mortgage and general upkeep on the property.

3. Leverage. Leverage means using a little of your money and a lot of someone else's money to make an investment—borrowing. A principal difference between real estate and other investment alternatives is the extensive use of leverage. Real estate is rarely bought outright with cash from the buyer's own pocket. In fact, there are several different lending institutions and financing techniques designed to accommodate real estate investors. The importance of leverage for real estate transactions is exemplified in the problem at the end of this chapter.

4. Security. If investment security is the primary objective of an investor, federal obligations (Treasury bills, Treasury bonds, etc.) may be the only way to go. However, if you are interested in growth, increases in income with minimum risks, and inflation protection, then real estate investing should be considered as part of your portfolio.

5. Passive appreciation. Growth is always an important objective when considering a real estate investment because values can rise with the expansion of a nearby community. For example, it is not unusual to find, near the boundaries of any large city, a tract of privately owned land that was purchased for $100 dollars an acre some years ago and is worth $100,000 an acre today. Such phenomenal growth, though, is a result of the expansion of a city and not due to the efforts of the owner. Time is always a major factor when growth is an objective in investing.

6. Matching income with rising costs. As maintenance, taxes, and other costs increase, a landlord is able to pass these expenses on to tenants. And, if interest rates rise, a landlord can invest rental deposits to take advantage of the increase.

7. Degree of involvement. Very few investment alternatives allow investors the opportunity to directly participate in manangement. Real estate not only permits active involvement, it also lets the investor choose the degree to which he or she will participate.If you have a way with landscaping but can't tell the difference between a wrench and a screwdriver, then fashion your plants the way you want, and leave the maintenance to professionals. If your schedule does not permit any involvement, then let a real estate management company take over the chores. (See Chapter 5 on "active participant" requirements for the availability of deductible losses.) At any rate, the degree of involvement is flexible according to your terms.

8. Pride in ownership. It is truly an American tradition to own land. Whether it is a vine-covered cottage in the country, a ranch-style house in the suburbs, or 100 acres of barren farm land near a city, ownership is considered the American way. After you are nestled in your own home, the next step is to purchase investment property.

9. The ability to structure a deal. Many times the structure of an investment in other areas is restricted (e.g., buying stocks on margin). Generally, the only restrictions on a real estate deal are those placed by the parties themselves. For example, if one fellow wants to sell his land to another for a 20-year promissory note at 9 percent interest without a down payment, so be it.

10. Income taxes. There always have been and there probably always will be tax laws accommodating real estate ownership. Depreciation, deductions for interest and operating costs, installment sales, and the ability to exchange property without tax liability still favor real estate investing.

DISADVANTAGES

Too bad we could not end right here, but unfortunately there are some very important disadvantages to real estate investing. You may personally have some to add to our list.

1. Recession/Depression. Real estate values tend to decline during such periods, which means the value of your portfolio is adversely affected. (See "Reverse Leverage" at the end of this chapter.) Although values are lower and sales are few, this is definitely a good period in which to seek out bargains if you have the capital to hold your find.

2. Liquidity. An investor may be concerned over whether he can *quickly convert* his holdings into cash without suffering a loss (liquidity). While there is a market for real estate, it may take some time to sell a property, especially if a sale at or near the market value is desired. Sometimes it takes a year or even longer to find a ready, willing and able buyer for a property. Only lucky investors have a qualified buyer on hand when their property goes up for sale. However, careful planning and managing of finances, could greatly reduce or possibly eliminate the time-lag disadvantages.

3. Amount invested. In most instances, a buyer must part with some of his own cash to purchase real estate. If a person plans to earn enough to support himself or his family from investment income, a rather large sum will be required. The alternative is retaining another means of support until the returns from the investment are sufficient to maintain a livelihood. Nevertheless, when a venture proves successful, you could easily stop working in your present position and take over the day-to-day management of your real estate investments.

4. Management. Investments in real estate generally involve income-producing properties such as multiple-family dwellings or shopping centers. After the purchase, these must be maintained and managed. Even if an investor is capable of performing these duties, he will probably still need the help of outside professionals to keep up with repairs, maintenance, landscaping, taxes, legal concerns, marketing, cash-flow, and similar specialized problems. Small investments require the same management abilities, but on a much smaller scale.

5. Accounting. Keeping a continuous eye on the financial situation requires the efforts of skilled personnel. Without a reasonably good record-keeping system, it would be impossible to make appropriate manangement decisions. Believe it or not, many ventures fail only because the participants did not spend the time or money necessary to provide the needed accounting reports.

6. Changing tax laws. Perhaps no other investment is so sensitive to even a slight tax-law adjustment as real estate. Even if Congress merely proposes a change in taxes, most investors will wait for the outcome before making a final decision, which will keep potential buyers from purchasing your property until the law is certain (and then, if it's unfavorable, they won't buy).

7. Financing. Not only can the investor's ability to come up with the required down payment be a drawback, but qualifying for a large enough loan can also present a problem. The lender wants to see stability, verifiable adequate income, collateral, and good credit history. However, there are ways to work within these constraints.

8. Miscellaneous. Changes in local zoning ordinances can affect the value of your investment. Deed restrictions, uncooperative neighbors, changes in traffic patterns, even the prospects of locating a nuclear disposal site nearby can also influence the real estate market.

One of the advantages of real estate investing listed above was leverage. Its impact on profitability is enormous. When appropriately used, leverage can have a multiplier effect in that a small cash investment can control a tremendous amount of capital and result in fantastic profits. The exercise below exemplifies this effect.

PROBLEM I — The Effect of Leverage

You are interested in putting $11,000 of hard-earned cash into an investment, and you have narrowed the alternatives down to either stocks or real estate. You can buy 1,100 shares of Acme Corporation stock for $10 a share (including brokerage commission)—$11,000 total cost (no dividends to be received). The other choice is income property—a duplex—costing $110,000, where the owner is willing to take 10 percent down and finance the rest at 11 percent. (Rentals exactly offset operating costs and debt service so that there is no net income received.) Assume both assets increase in value at a rate of 15 percent in one year and you sell at that point in time. What is your rate of return before income taxes on (1) the stock and (2) the real estate? (Assume that the real estate is sold via an installment sale without a real estate broker getting involved; ignore the depreciation expense deduction on the duplex; use the simple rate of return formula for exactly one year = profit/cost; and assume no points and very slight closing costs—say, less than $400—are involved.)

Answer:

Stocks

Selling Price	$12,650	[(11,000 × .15) + 11,000]
Cost	(11,000)	
Profit	$1,650	

Rate of Return = 15% (Profit/Cost or $1,650/$11,000)

Duplex

Selling Price	$126,500	[($110,000 × .15) + $110,000]
Cost	(110,000)	
Profit	$16,500	

Rate of Return = 150% (Profit/Cost or $16,500/$11,000)

Excited? You should be. Leverage is the most dynamic and mis-understood element in real estate investing. Your $11,000 investment more than doubled in one year if you bought the duplex, but you only experienced a 15 percent return on the stock—yet the value of both investments grew at precisely the same rate. And there was a tax benefit from a depreciation deduction on the duplex! If the terms of the installment sale provided 10 percent down, then *at least* $12,650 would be received in the year of sale.

REVERSE LEVERAGE

Before you rush out and purchase something using leverage, per-haps you should see its other side. Leverage is a wonderful tool, but like everything else it has its drawbacks. Make a bad deal here and it can be downright devastating. Take, for example, the same facts as before except that both investments lose 10 percent of their value at the end of the year, how would you stand then? The value of the stocks will be $9,900, and you could sell them and simply buy something else with the proceeds. The value of the duplex, on the other hand, will drop to $99,000, and you will lose every cent (more if you wound up paying some professional fees) of your initial investment if it were sold at that price. This is an example of "reverse leverage."

Chapter
One

INVESTMENT PLANNING

Achieving success in an investment venture is merely a matter of reaching the objective for which the investment was made—fulfilling the investment plan or strategy. Unsuccessful investing can be directly attributed to a poorly designed investment strategy, improperly implementing a strategy, or not having a definite strategy (plan) at all. A real estate investor, like any other investor, must begin with a detailed plan for the purpose of defining, attaining, and maintaining successful investments.

The first step in developing a formal strategy is to identify and define your overall investment philosophy. Next you must clarify and refine your objectives. And the last step is to devise attainable goals which lead to accomplishing the objective. Such a plan must be flexible because circumstances change, thereby changing your philosophy, which in turn will alter your objective and goals. Devising a formal plan will not eliminate the need for intuition and quick decisions, nor will it compensate for faulty judgment, but it will help to reduce the number and severity of blunders.

INVESTMENT PHILOSOPHY

All investors, whether or not they are conscious of it, have an investment philosophy. It is derived from beliefs, knowledge, principles,

and desires for attaining certain financial objectives. Many philosophies, however, are not well-defined. ''Making a reasonable profit
in the shortest possible time without incurring undue risk'' is almost
everyone's overall investment goal, but it is not specific enough to
provide a clear direction. Given all variables and constraints, a more
precise philosophy must be identified. Although flexibility is important, adhering to a specific investment strategy will improve an
investor's position by focusing his or her energy and efforts toward
a clear-cut objective.

The purpose of explicitly defining an investment philosophy, then,
is to provide a distinct basis for developing investment strategies.
A well-defined philosophy serves as a pervasive guideline for for-
mulating not only strategies, but objectives, goals, and other plans
as well. It takes into consideration what an investor is after and
influences how this will be attained.

In determining an investment philosophy, all of the factors listed
in Exhibit 1-1 (p. 24) must be evaluated. Perhaps the most critical
factors are an investor's primary and secondary financial objectives,
such as future income, value appreciation, preserving purchasing
power, and/or cash flow. A second important factor is the level of
risk a person is willing to assume. For example, the older an investor is, generally, the less risk he or she is willing to tolerate. In
addition, the amount of available money to invest, specific knowledge, direct involvement, and time commitment are extremely influential and must also be carefully weighed.

Value Appreciation—In the past, equity buildup (value appreciation) was always an important characteristic of real estate investment.
Purchasing property at today's prices and selling at tomorrow's
values has proven to be one of the best incentives for purchasing
real property. Even though values rise, appreciation is not taxed until
the property is disposed of (and, in some cases, not even then).
Because value appreciation is virtually always a factor in real estate
investment, it will either be the primary or a secondary objective.
When appreciation is the primary objective, though, leverage is customarily used to purchase the property, which will enhance the rate
of return when the investment is sold. A property's appreciation
in value is generally viewed as a long-term proposition: A property
is purchased for a reasonable price and so many years later it is sold

for a tidy profit.

Cash Flow—If cash flow is an investor's primary objective, rental properties purchased using more equity and less leverage are a desirable vehicle. A fairly large amount of cash is usually required, and such projects are typically managed by the owner. The basic strategy is to purchase properties using little or no leverage and receive most or all the rental payments. For example, you purchase a $70,000 rental property outright (i.e., without a loan) and receive $680 a month in rent. With a 10 percent vacancy/credit loss rate and $800 a year maintenance expenses and property taxes, you would experience about a 9.3 percent pretax return on your investment (not including appreciation).

Purchasing Power—If a person wants to guard against the erosion of his or her purchasing power, real estate appreciates in value during inflationary periods, usually at a faster rate than inflation. If the property is leveraged, the owner's equity also gradually increases.

Future Income—Perhaps future income is what an investor seeks. One strategy is to buy new rental houses with a 15-year mortgage. After the mortgage is paid off, the investor is able to enjoy all income from rentals, perhaps as a retirement income. Purchasing 10 homes in this manner over an extended period will certainly provide substantial retirement benefits that will quickly adjust to inflationary pressures. On the other hand, if the after-tax value of the homes outweighs the amount of rentals to be received at retirement (in terms of prevailing interest rates), then the properties could be sold under the installment sales method using the prevailing rate of interest for long-term mortgages. For purposes of evaluating cash flow, then, saving some money now through rental-property tax deductions while the property owner is still in a higher tax bracket, and at the same time amortizing the outstanding debt with rental receipts, is certainly an excellent method of acquiring retirement income. This objective is especially enhanced if your tax bracket will be lower after retirement.

Estate Building—Building an estate can also be accomplished through increasing equity. Generally, this too, is a long-term objective that normally requires a considerable amount of time and capital—more than when mere value appreciation is the goal. Certain properties, such as well-maintained buildings and even ''raw'' (undeveloped) land, are sought for such purposes. The objective calls for purchasing properties and subsequently holding them so that equity will increase (which in turn increases the value of an estate). Whenever estate building is an objective, however, cash flow is typically not considered to be of major importance.

Diversification—Real property offers a diversification to securities investors and others because real estate values tend to respond differently to economic conditions—they may offer a hedge. For example, in the recent past the stock market did not perform particularly well during inflationary periods, but real estate values as a whole consistently rose. In addition, diversification can also be obtained within a real estate portfolio by acquiring houses in different neighborhoods and different price ranges. Large national real estate investment companies diversify by investing in different localities across the nation.

Use—Another investment plan can involve purchasing property for use. As an example, an investor bought a very nice, expensive home in a remote resort. His plan is to rent it out for approximately 10 years and then make it his principal residence at retirement. In the meantime, he receives the tax benefits of rental property ownership, debt service (mortgage payments) can be covered by the rental income, and by the time the residence is ready for his occupancy, the monthly mortgage will likely be more affordable, especially with a retirement income. This plan will work extremely well if inflation flares back up. Also note that refinancing at more favorable rates is always an alternative during periods when interest rates are low.

Immediate Profits—If immediate profits are sought, then purchase properties that can be quickly sold for a profit—easy to say, but this plan requires quite a bit of expertise, skill, and fortitude. Seeking immediate profits is perhaps the riskiest objective. Some "talented" investors become very sophisticated as to what is desirable in a given area. These people search for properties that have been on the market for a long time and plan to make cosmetic changes once the investment is acquired for a bargain price. These cosmetic changes turn an otherwise undesirable property into a fast, profitable seller. Usually, just after such property is acquired, it is immediately rented for one year or less, if it is inhabitable, while the landscaping/ refurbishing begins. After reconstruction, the property will be on the market again for a higher price. In some instances, the tenants wind up buying it.

The immediate-profits-type investor seeks lower-priced homes in higher-priced neighborhoods. He or she is also looking for houses that need a reasonable and necessary amount of work (using contractors to estimate the costs prior to purchasing). The investor must also be absolutely certain that there are no incurable problems which are out of a property owner's control—economic obsolescence which will keep a property's value low, such as extraneous nuisances (e.g., a nearby airport or nuclear plant), changes in zoning laws (e.g., an industrial complex will be built next to the property's subdivision), or changes in surroundings (e.g., a well-maintained house in a deteriorating neighborhood). Obviously, economic obsolescence is always a concern, but it is crucial in this type of investing.

RISK TOLERANCE   The amount of risk you are willing to assume is another factor to be considered. Generally, risk is the probability that an investment will not be profitable. Some investments are virtually riskless because the returns are guaranteed when the puchase is made. U.S. government Treasury bills are an example. Other investments, such as commodity futures, are very high risk because they are subject to great fluctuations in price over relatively short periods of time. Certain forms of real estate carry less risk than others, and single-family residences are, for the most part, in the ''less risk'' category.

The other side of risk tolerance is the *return* from an investment. Generally, the lower the risk, the lower the return. Without considering location and other extraneous factors, lower risk real estate projects typically involve existing properties already having high-quality tenants with favorable long-term leases. Conversely, high-risk projects are those still on the drawing board without any prospective tenants in sight.

Risk and rate of return are also influenced by price in that acquiring a property for an amount below its fair market value will tend to decrease the risk of loss, while at the same time increasing its probable rate of return. Paying too high a price increases the risk of loss in that the odds are against your getting back your purchase price, much less a profit, upon eventual sale.

An investor who demands high returns and is willing to take on high-risk projects requiring large amounts of cash, skill, direct involvment, and time will develop a vastly different investment strategy from one who wishes to avoid risk and large, time-consuming projects. Because the two philosophies are different, these investors will probably not look for similar properties.

Although there are many ways to describe one's philosophy in terms of risk tolerance and individual objectives, three major categories are used here. They are aggressive, moderate, and low risk. The designations, however, are only used to identify the types of property that each level would search for and are not intended to be a applied as rigid rules for determining your level of willingness to assume risk.

Aggressive—An aggressive philosophy is one that seeks high profits in a relatively short period of time, which in return, calls for purchasing high-risk projects, usually at fair market value using maximum leverage. Normally, cash flow is not a requisite feature, and a high level of skill is needed. The property's value increases as improvements are made. Once the project is operating or the building is completed, it is to be sold immediately. Buying raw land and constructing a building for the purpose of leasing to unsigned tenants and then selling the entire project, for example, is considered to be extremely high risk, especially in a barren locale where prospective tenants do not appear to be readily available. The payoff here can be tremendous if a favorable tenant relationship is developed and surrounding values rapidly appreciate from the anticipated type of growth. Buying an old structure in a run-down neighborhood to refurbish and lease to unsigned tenants also involves high risk. An investor attempting to rehabilitate an old structure under such conditions is anticipating a neighborhood turnaround, which is very risky and may take quite a while, but the property will return a handsome profit should the event take place.

Moderate—A moderate philosophy involves seeking existing properties which are not yet rented in a fairly good neighborhood for a price at or near fair market value. The property is to be leveraged and kept for a longer period than an aggressive philosophy would involve. Cash flow may or may not be a required element, but it is not particularly important initially. Using 80 percent leverage to buy a residence in reasonably good surroundings and that is to be held eight years, for example, is not as risky as developing a property to be sold immediately. The former, therefore, carries a moderate amount of risk. However, the building may be in need of some repair. Value appreciation over an extended period is the fundamental basis for this type of investment.

Low—A low-risk philosophy (also known as a "turnkey philosophy") is one that involves acquiring existing properties which already have favorable leases, at prices below fair market value. The neighborhoods must be well established; the structures must be sound and well maintained. Typically, the property is to be held for a long period of time and cash flow sometimes is the primary consideration, even though value will normally appreciate. Some feel that a lesser amount of leverage may provide less risk. This may be true in some cases, if property values decline. However, when a *nonrecourse* loan is involved, risk is substantially reduced in that only the down payment is "at risk." Thus, if a 10 percent down project is undertaken with nonrecourse financing, the investor stands to lose only the amount paid down and no more. (See "At Risk Rules" in Chapter 5.)

OTHER FACTORS Obviously, the amount of money to be invested is important because it will tend to eliminate some properties. Your knowledge and the amount of involvement required (i.e., passive investor versus active property manager/owner) will also dictate the types of properties to be purchased. (As we suggested before, those who are not familiar with rental properties should start with single-family homes.) Finally, the amount of time committed to real estate investing must be addressed, including strategy development, property selection, property acquisitions and maintenance, and disposition of the property. Other unique constraints on a more personal level, such as a physical impairment, will also play a role.

In order to begin and continue profitable real estate investing, certain significant items should be established in all real estate philosophies including:

(a). *Customer satisfaction.* Sellers, renters, or buyers should never feel cheated or swindled. This requires tact, integrity, and public relations skills.

(b). *Community considerations.* What will be the impact on the community where a rental house is located? Will such property be maintained? From the investor's standpoint, it should enhance the community and certainly not debase it.

Exhibit 1-1
Investment Philosophy Factors

*Primary/Secondary Financial Objectives:
    1. Value appreciation
    2. Cash flow
    3. Preserving purchasing power
    4. Future income
    5. Estate building
    6. Diversification
    7. Use of investment
    8. Immediate profits
    9. Other

*Level of Risk Tolerance:
    1. Aggressive
    2. Moderate
    3. Low

*Available Cash

*Level of Sophistication:
    1. Quite knowledgeable
    2. Somewhat informed
    3. Novice

*Amount of Involvement:
    1. Active manager
    2. Passive investor

*Time to be Committed

*Other Considerations

CLARIFY AND REFINE OBJECTIVES

After identifying an investment philosophy, the objectives, which were already considered, can now be more clearly developed. As previously mentioned, an objective is the overall purpose for investing; it must be specific, realistic, and attainable. Then the goals, which are the details of the plan, can be drawn up. A fully developed strategy serves as a guide for portfolio selection in that all "accept/reject" criteria are well established before any properties are evaluated.

When a property can be acquired for a price well below market value, it may be possible to completely leverage the property and still generate cash flow, which in this case, would be a secondary objective. For example, assume your level of risk is moderate, and you are primarily interested in appreciation. You plan to patiently wait for a below-market deal (thereby lowering risk) and to use maximum leverage. You finally find a property worth $100,000 in a nice area. It was listed for $88,000 and had been on the market for a couple of years, yet a motivated seller accepted your offer of $76,000! You also found a mortgage company willing to finance the entire purchase price (which falls within 80 percent of its fair market value) at 10 percent for 30 years. Monthly PITI (principal, interest, taxes, and insurance) is $985; it will rent for $1,200 a month after making some minor improvements. Note that in this example the investment provides cash flow, but this was not the primary objective.

As stated previously, if cash flow is a primary objective, then usually a large amount of equity is required. One retired lady, who was in a very low income tax bracket, was getting ready to sell her home until she found out it could be leased for quite a sum. She had purchased it 27 years ago for $42,000 and pays monthly PITI of $366 (with three years remaining). Recently the home was valued at $250,000 (i.e., equity of around $240,000) and she rented it easily for $2,400 a month. Because only a small amount of cash flow was needed to supplement her retirement income, the residence was converted into rental property by turning it over to a property management company; she moved into a fashionable apartment. She will experience a return of approximately 9 percent before income taxes just from cash flow, and the property will probably continue to appreciate in value.

GOALS

Goals are the short-run steps that enable an investor to reach his or her investment objectives. They are usually specific and financially oriented, but sometimes are general and nonfinancial. Goals are outlined in considerable detail and state how an investor intends to accomplish his or her mission within a given time frame and the point at which the objectives are achieved and the activity is terminated or adjusted.

SAMPLE STRATEGY   Assume you have a moderate tolerance for risk and your objective is to retire in 15 years, thereby supplementing your retirement income with income derived from real estate investing. You have $15,000 with which to work, have purchased three residences in the past, and are willing to spend some time to locate, purchase, and maintain potential investment properties.

Your goals include searching for and buying one rental property within six months. It must have at least three bedrooms, two baths, a fireplace, a family room, a two-car garage, and be located in a nice neighborhood. The price cannot be more than $125,000, unless favorable terms can be worked out with the seller. For the first two months you plan to initially search without a real estate agent, but another goal is to find an agent that can locate the types of properties you are seeking, is aware of the potential growth and undesirable localities as well as current trends, is knowledgeable in the area of property investment and management, and is willing to provide help after a sale is made (e.g., recommending individuals such as plumbers, carpet layers, roofers, etc., who provide good service).

If a suitable property is not found during the first 60 days, then real estate agents, perhaps no more than three, will be used until you find an agent you will work with again even if you do not buy the first investment through him or her. During the search, local classified ads are to be skimmed and designated neighborhoods are to be watched for properties that may be available for below market prices (to decrease risks), for foreclosed property auctions; for owners who are in a hurry to sell (i.e., motivated sellers); or for properties that have been on the market for an extended period of time and have not sold because they do not show well but can be "dressed up" for a reasonable cost. The total purchase price including fixing-up expenditures is not to exceed 85 percent of the property's fair market value.

After you hold the property for at least four years, it is to be sold, and with the profits, two more houses are to be acquired under somewhat similar conditions. (By this time you will be well acquainted with real estate investing in your area.) After four more years, one or both of the houses will be sold and with the profits, two more houses are to be acquired—the actual number of sales will be determined at that time. Thus, in 8-10 years you plan to own three or four houses through a form of pyramiding (i.e., using profits from homes sold to purchase more properties).

An alternative strategy would be to hold on to all "good" properties—those most likely to increase in value—and purchase more properties by using funds from other sources, such as from a designated savings account or other profitable investments. By telling your real estate agent that you are always in the market for a good prospect, you can easily stay in touch with market developments and can sometimes find a real gem.

After 15 years, all properties are to be evaluated in terms of after-tax cash flow and appreciation, with regard to keeping or selling some or all of them and placing the money into other cash-generating investments.

Notice that the philosophy and objectives were identified and the goals were stated in detail. The stategy outlines a clear picture of what it is you are searching for and puts you in an excellent position to focus on the type of properties that can most likely meet your objective. It has defined the parameters of your investment activities and has given you a road map not only for finding one property, but for locating a suitable real estate agent as well.

Below-market properties have been emphasized in the examples so far because they tend to be less risky over the long run. Many sophisticated investors, however, seek properties that they think will increase in value in a relatively short period or plan to hold on to ones that are believed to be quite marketable, rather than spending time looking for a bargain. As your knowledge increases, your philosophy will change.

STUDIES AND ANALYSIS

Using outside independent sources may help in the development of a strategy because they provide some insight into expected conditions for an area can be an effective tool for planning. Such sources include feasibility studies, market analysis, and marketability analysis. Although the studies and analyses are rather sophisticated and usually quite expensive, they are sometimes available to individual investors for little or no cost through a local planning commission, real estate consulting firm, real estate broker, or development company that previously used it. These studies and analyses involve the following:

1. The feasibility study, also known as the feasibility analysis, focuses on the future by attempting to answer the questions, "Is this particular project likely to succeed?" "If so, what are the problems it is likely to encounter?" and "If not, why not?" These studies are not infallible, but they do provide much factual information about the probability of success in terms of financial and nonfinancial data. In Chapter 4 we will discuss financial feasibility analysis in much more detail.

2. The market study and analysis. The market study is designed to reveal the localized market that may (or may not) exist for a given type of property. The analysis looks to the future by attempting to determine the prospects for further demand in the area. These studies are quite important for an investor interested in development or related services, but can also be a valuable tool for investors in single-family houses who have an investment plan for expansion and growth.

3. The marketability study determines the overall acceptance or rejection of the use of a specific property by the market. It is most important to a developer or someone going into business. It also has value for an investor intending to put his cash in the rental market for single-family houses, especially if the

investment strategy calls for going into neighborhoods that have no other rentals.

4. The risk analysis. What are the risks involved in an investment venture in real estate? Of course, no answer can be specific and definite, but a good study, usually called a risk analysis, can provide quite a bit of information on what may be expected. The study generally gives the probability of a variety of events that can affect the value of an investment. Although risks cannot be completely avoided, their occurrence must be planned for and proper risk manangement must be employed in order to avoid losing on the investment.

The list of studies pertaining to real estate investment presented here is not complete; there are no accepted or approved titles for each of these studies as they are often written for a specific project with its own peculiar problems. However, we have selected what we think are the most descriptive titles for studies that are frequently used for investing in real estate.

Chapter
Two

GETTING STARTED

Investing in projects with which you are not already familiar calls for the aid of an expert, a person who is willing to provide his or her time and knowledge to help you accomplish your objective. If you do not have a trustworthy friend or relative in the business who is easy to work with and willing to help, find a real estate broker or agent who will provide their services. Be sure the broker or agent is truly knowledgeable in real estate investing. We recommend such individuals because their success is dependent on your success, so your problems will be their problems. They can usually provide answers for many questions when you won't even know where to look for information.

You will need someone who is available to answer all kinds of questions, such as "who is the best real estate attorney for handling a zoning matter in the city of Clarksdale?" "Who currently offers the best financial package for investors?" Or "where is the next major development going to take place?" Even after your initial purchases, you may still want to stay in touch with and use the services of a knowledgeable real estate professional to keep up-to-date on current events and to help find or sell your properties.

Real estate agencies are established by state law and involve at least one broker who, on rare occasions, may operate alone or who has one or more salespersons acting for him or her. These salespeople mostly deal with the public and are authorized to list and sell real estate as agents of a broker; they are not entitled to list or sell independently. Listing refers to accepting property at the request of an owner for the purpose of finding a ready, willing, and able buyer under conditions set forth by the owner in a listing contract.

HELP

In searching for your first "investment" house, get the help of an agent or broker who is or has been in rental property management, preferably one who has already been successful in investing in similar properties. Ask around. In some cases, the Yellow Pages lists brokers who manage rental properties.

Once you have a lead, give the agent or broker a call and ask about his or her experience in management and investment activities. During this call, be sure to provide only a limited amount of information concerning the types of property you are seeking and make an appointment for an office visit to discuss your project in more detail. At this stage, you are "qualifying" the broker or agent. Be aware, however, that there are always a few brokers or agents who also invest in residential property and may be a little reluctant to reveal the information you need. Avoid them; there are many more who would be quite willing to help. Also note that there are quite a few in the profession who are not qualified to work with this type of property, but are quite willing to respond as if they were: Avoid them too! If you sense that the broker or agent is not qualified, perhaps he or she can refer you to someone who specializes in investing in single-family homes.

Most brokers do not actively engage in selling; they will, instead, refer you to a salesperson. An ideal situation would be to work closely with a knowledgeable broker, who, in turn, allows a new agent to show the properties. In this way you get the expertise of the broker and the services of a salesperson. Some salespeople also possess a broker's license and generally have much more experience than a novice, but they still act as agents for the broker they represent. These individuals may be perfect for your project or may be too busy with other clients and their own property to work with an investor. At any rate, the managing broker should be able to personally help out or place you with a qualified salesperson who can perform as desired. We therefore recommend starting with a managing broker.

Either the agent or the broker will ask many questions on the first visit in an effort to qualify you as a potential buyer, and to find out exactly what types of property to show. Because you already have an investment strategy, you are now in an excellent position to discuss in detail the types of property you wish to purchase. Before viewing any property, however, tell the salesperson about your philosophy and objectives and ask for his or her opinion as to whether the types of property you are looking for will accomplish your goals in light of current trends in the local market. You may find a different approach which could very well lead to a constructive modification of your strategy; at least you should get a better idea of whether this person is going to be able to do the job.

Information an investor can expect from the salesperson includes the following:

1. *Location*—Information on single-family-home neighborhoods, rental market demands within different price ranges, community growth patterns, and current and expected trends in style and layout.

2. *Legality*—Application of state laws and local ordinances relating to rental property, landlords, and tenants, as well as existing documents that will be needed.

3. *Appraisal*—Features to look for in property that will enhance or hinder the rental potential, and features that tend to enhance the overall value.

4. *Financing*—Sources of mortgage money for investment in rental houses and current trends in imaginative financing; all items that will be needed at or before closing.

5. *Quick Title Search*—How to find the owner of a particular piece of property. (The person who pays the property tax, as shown in the county tax records, is usually the owner.) Where and how to check on possible liens recorded on a property, including mechanic's, tax, mortgage, and judgment liens (see Glossary).

6. *Unanticipated Problems*—Many questions seem to arise that a real estate professional can answer. Examples include: problems to expect from renters other than nonpayment of rent; how to handle

certain aspects of advertising, managing, and maintaining the property. You may even decide to use the agency's property management service rather than managing the property yourself.

EXAMINING PROPERTY

The ideal property an investor will be looking for as the first unit should be priced at or lower than fair market value, located in an area where rental demands are high, in an excellent state of repair, and owned by a person who is ready to sell this afternoon.

If you do not find any houses to your liking the first couple of times out, feel free to look for another agency. It may take quite a while to find something that is suitable, but do not be in a hurry; do not look at more than four houses a day. Be sure to keep records—on each house you visit, by address. Should a house ever come up again, you will be able to locate the facts and comments you have already made. Otherwise, it is difficult to keep in mind all the peculiarities of every house visited. Use the checklist in Exhibit 2–1 (p. 37) as a starting point; adjust it in terms of your objectives and goals. If you have the address and a detailed description of each house, you know precisely what to focus on in case you decide later to take another look and to compare it with the more interesting prospects; on the other hand, if you do not wish to pursue a house any further, you will know to avoid this address.

Upon first arriving at a house, immediately notice its overall appearance: style, color, windows, sidewalks, potential maintenance problems, etc. Your first impression is extremely important. Is it on a busy street or a cul-de-sac? Is it close to shopping centers, schools, churches, playgrounds, etc.? What is the neighborhood like? What is the possibility that the property will be rezoned for commercial use? Ask the agent. On the inside, observe everything, again, using your first impression; especially notice the layout. Are there any signs of economic obsolescence? Ask yourself—and the salesperson—what it will take (other than rezoning) for this house to quickly sell at fair market value and make a note of it.

Not all houses can be easily sold at fair market value. A house that stands out and is quite different from all other houses in the

---

Exhibit 2–1
Checklist for Single-Family Rental Homes

GENERAL
- Address
- Date
- Asking price
- Age
- Style (Ranch, Traditional, Cape Cod, Victorian, Tudor, Custom, Contemporary, Mediterranean, Spanish, Georgian, Other)
- Owner's name (title vested in)
- Owner's address and phone
- Existing rental agreement?
  - Property operated by owner/property mgr.?
  - Acquisition date
  - Length of existing agreement
- How long has it been listed? At what price?
- Reason for selling
- Who to call to inspect property
- Date to be vacated

PROXIMITY TO
- Public transportation
- Shopping areas
- Schools (day care, grammar, jr. high, high, parochial, colleges)
- Churches
- Recreational facilities
- Public nuisances (airport, freeways, parking lots, etc.)
- Other

STRUCTURE
- Exterior (type, condition, & color)
- Stories
- Type of roof & condition
- Sewer (septic tank, public, other)
- Heating (elec., gas, solar, oil, wood stoves, etc.)
- Air conditioning (central or window)
- Attic fan
- Flooring (types & condition)

- Quality of insulation
- Weatherstripping
- Storm windows
- Window screens
- Plumbing (copper, plastic, galvanized)
- Wiring (type 110/220 volt & condition)
- Washer/dryer hookup (elec. or gas)
- Cable TV
- Basement
- Garage (no. of cars)
- Available storage area
- Home protection program
- Foundation
- Outside lighting
- Other

LAND
- Separate appraised value
- Lot size
- Zoning
- View (front & back)
- Patio/Deck
- Street improvements (sidewalks, street lights, etc.)
- Condition of yard
- Fencing
- Corner
- Other

INTERIOR
- Overall condition
- Square footage
- Bedrooms (size, closet space and number, electrical outlets, windows, etc.)
- Full bathrooms (showers, tubs, garden tubs, etc.)
- Living room
- Family room
- Breakfast room
- Kitchen—stove & oven (gas or elec.), disposal, dishwasher, refrigerator, microwave, other
- Laundry room (gas or elec. hookup)
- Fireplace/wood-burning stove

- Draperies
- Carpeting
- Personal property extras
- Improvements required
- Other

FINANCING
- Earnest money deposit
- Down payment
- Total amount due at closing
- Existing loan transferable?
    - Loan balance
    - Monthly payments (PITI)
    - Lender's name and address
    - Loan number
    - Assumption fee
    - Can be taken "subject to?"
    - Balloon payment (due date)
    - Interest portion for next 12 months
    - Prepayment penalty
- New loan amount
    - Loan commitment fee & terms
    - Monthly payments (PI)
    - Lender's name and address
    - Interest rate
    - Points (locked in or floating)
    - Private mortgage insurance (PMI) or FHA
- Seller pays closing costs?
- Seller pays points?
- Seller financing?
    - Amount
    - Interest rate
    - Number of years
    - Monthly payment (PI)
    - Due date
    - Blended rate
    - Special terms
- Annual property taxes (T)
- Annual insurance premium (I)

OTHER EXPECTED COSTS
- Maintenance (recurring)
  - Painting/Wallpapering
  - Yard
  - Pest control
  - Other
- Repairs
  - Roof
  - Interior/exterior walls, windows, doors
  - Plumbing
  - Electrical
  - Structural
  - Other
- Improvements to be made
  - Additions
  - Conversions
  - Other

---

neighborhood probably will not be a good candidate to purchase. The very house you personally like may be one that will not sell quickly. An experienced salesperson can really help in this regard. Your skill in appraising potential purchases will quickly be enhanced by working with an experienced professional.

Before you discuss your notes with the salesperson, get as much information as you can from the agent or the owner about potential rental income, expected maintenance costs, estimated cost of needed repairs, the neighborhood, and anything else that comes to mind about this house. Ask for the names of reputable home-improvement companies. (These companies are often the best source for estimates on all kinds of repairs.)

At this point, ignore your personal feelings about any unit that has been inspected. Assuming the house already has value-appreciation potential, the one question you are always concerned with is, ''Will someone choose to live in this house for a monthly rental that I must receive if I purchase it at the asking price?'' The answer will depend on the property's price and terms, especially how much down and how much per month will be required. The salesperson should know the current mortgage rates for institutional loans and be able to quickly figure an approximate monthly payment. If the seller is willing to finance part or all of the purchase price, then a quick comparison between the institutions' and the seller's terms can be made.

Do not buy the first house you inspect no matter how good it looks. If you get a strong feeling that this is *the* house, ignore it, initially. You must inspect a number of houses before making a decision to buy. Where time and finances permit, look at several houses in other neighborhoods and in different price ranges before making a first buy. Keeping detailed records on each unit you visit will make your decision easier, not only for the first house purchased but for all the others as well.

As you inspect houses, look for the one that comes closest to meeting your objectives and goals. Probably the simplest way to do this is to use a checklist that is custom-made from your strategy. Comparisons between each of the houses can be made quite easily using the list, and it will help keep you from overlooking something relevant. Use the checklist in Exhibit 2–1 and adjust it according to your specifications.

Make a copy of Exhibit 2–1 for each house you inspect. Customize it by highlighting and/or adding items that are necessary in a single-family house according to your ''investment'' standards and your agent's suggestions. This is important because each area is different and certain features are almost absolutely necessary for a house to sell. For example, in a particular area of the country, a full, finished basement is virtually a requisite feature for a house to sell quickly; you can expect a home without a basement to stay on the market for a longer period of time. Your agent should know this.

Putting in a basement may not be financially feasible, but something like a fireplace or garden tub may be. Certain below-market prospects that you are considering may be improved by putting in such items. Your agent may feel that not having such an important component is one of the reasons the house has not already sold. Or the property may be in need of painting, wallpapering, landscaping, etc., which means it does not ''show'' well. At any rate, adjusting your checklist to reflect such variables will make it easier as you consider properties.

Also note that if a major improvement, such as installing a fireplace, were needed, you could get an estimate of its total cost and incorporate the amount in your checklist. You will do this for all properties visited, so that a comparison can be made between the properties. By weighing the advantages and disadvantages of each house in like manner, you improve your chances of making a good decision.

Before deciding to purchase a property, be sure to find out why an owner wants to sell. A seller who has a low-rate mortgage on about half the asking price and is selling to move to a larger, nicer house is likely to have a firm price because time is not ''of the essence.'' In contrast, a motivated seller is generally one who is forced to move and is willing to take a sizable reduction in order to unload the property. In this case there is typically a mortgage of at least 70 percent on the asking price.

Distressed sellers include those that can no longer afford to live in the house, a third party who only wants to liquidate the asset—usually by auction—as soon as possible (estates, mortgage insurers, mortgagees, etc.), individuals transferred to different areas and making monthly payments on two homes, divorced couples anxious to divide things up, and others who, for various personal reasons, are in a hurry and are ready to move. As a general rule, the longer a property has been on the market, the more willing an owner is to sell at a lower price, especially a motivated seller as described. These people need immediate relief, and your philosophy is to provide the necessary aid.

When you are ready to make an offer, the salesperson will complete a purchase agreement (or sales contract), which is your contract to buy and the owner's contract to deliver, as well as collect an earnest money deposit. The purchase agreement is a legal document that becomes binding as soon as both of you sign it. Because the buyer initiates the sale, you are in a position to specify all terms within the original agreement, such as the the sales price, a contingency upon finding specified financing, and who pays the closing costs, points, pest control inspection, and property taxes. It is good business practice to be familar with the preprinted form before you sign. You should be able to obtain a copy from your salesperson simply by asking for one.

NEGOTIATING

Negotiating is the key in obtaining satisfactory terms for financing the purchase. In order to be in a position to negotiate, however, a purchaser must never be in a hurry and must be ready to start the process by setting forth the initial terms, which tend to be in the buyer's favor.

One of the first items to be filled in on the purchase agreement is the total price you are offering, which should be less than the asking price when a third-party lender is to be used. If the seller is financing the project, however, then the asking price may stand, but the terms will be negotiable.

There are spaces in the purchase agreement for points and closing costs, usually with no distinction as to who will pay them. Therefore, they too, are negotiable, and you will want the seller to pay them. However, as the process continues and if you really want the property, then you might wind up paying at least a portion of the points and closing costs, but this is included as part of your strategy so there will be no suprises in the end.

Other items in the contract that may be used in negotiating are: the time allowed for the seller to make a decision, time for seller to vacate the property, and additional terms and conditions.

The buyer has the opportunity to specify the length of time allowed the owner to decide whether or not to accept the terms offered. Upon expiration, the purchase contract becomes null and void. If you are offering a substantially reduced price along with a reasonable down payment—enough to pay the broker's commission, closing costs, and points—it may be advisable to allow a very short time, such as 24 hours.

Many sellers, however, are very price conscious and will not even consider a lower price. A buyer can counter by dictating all other advantageous terms of the sale, such as financing, closing costs, points, painting, fencing, carpeting, landscaping, and any other adjustments. Warning! Whenever any such terms are added to a contract, be sure to specify *exactly* the type, color, brand, style, price, even a catalog number of the item or service you want because, without such specifications, the seller can—and will—find the cheapest available avenue out.

An added inducement to accept your offer is allowing the seller to stay in the house as a tenant until favorable relocating arrangements can be completed. The amount to be paid for rent is also negotiable and is dependent upon how badly you want the house and what is considered a reasonable amount of time for the seller to find another place to live. A seller who cannot afford to continue in a house, for example, may be quite willing to sell at favorable terms, but only if he or she can pay a reduced amount each month for a specified period, say six months. Such a move may initially reduce your cash flow, but you have helped the seller and obtained title to the house.

Whenever the offering price is significantly lower than the asking price, do not add any additional terms or conditions that make unduly harsh demands on the seller. This is your opportunity to make the seller feel that you are not cheating or mistreating him. You can specify such things as that the draperies are to stay (window treatment) and the house is to be clean and in good order after the owner moves, but you should not provide exact specifications of every adjustment you want to make to the house.

However, if you find that the buyer is strictly price conscious, then use the contract to specify a reasonable number of adjustments to compensate for the higher price. Consult with your salesperson about including other items that may increase the willingness of the seller to accept your offer without significantly increasing your cost.

A motivated seller will eventually come to realize that the asking price is too high for the condition of the home and that he or she is not in a particularly good position to negotiate for an extended period of time.

The owner may accept your initial offer, but in most cases he or she will make a counter offer. When the seller proposes any changes from your original contract, in effect, it becomes a new contract to which you are not bound. Should you agree to the changes, initial them: You will then become bound if all other necessary elements of a contract are present. Offers, counter offers, counter–counter offers, etc., can and usually do go back and forth until finally both parties either accept or reject.

Some property owners will get mad. Your original offer is so low or demanding that they become "insulted" by such "irresponsible audacity." A majority of these people will not even make a counter offer, which will immediately terminate the negotiation process because they are not the type of seller you are looking for and they probably will not sell to you, now, anyway. Do not waste time here. Find another seller but keep in mind that frivolous offers which are way too low will only make people upset; such offers will never accomplish your objective. Be prepared for somebody to be rubbed the wrong way even when you have made a "legitimate" offer.

Sellers who are only interested in selling the property will usually make a counter offer. At this point you must reassess how badly you want the property as well as the total amount you are willing to invest in order to bring the house up to your standard. Because the seller has the ability to make a counter offer, never put your "best offer" forward in the original purchase contract. Allow the seller to make his or her own deal in light of the circumstances influencing the sale, for which you have so patiently searched. Nevertheless, be absolutely certain as to the total amount you can possibly invest *before* making an offer.

After both seller and buyer have signed the purchase contract, the closing is the last major event that must take place before the property actually changes hands. The purchase contract is delivered to the attorney handling the closing. The attorney, in turn, makes sure that all items agreed to in the contract are performed, a title search has been made, and all other adjustments and activities pertaining to the transaction are complete. Then the final arrangements for title transfer from the present owner to the buyer are made. In addition, all payments associated with the transfer are made at closing. Be sure you are aware of the amount and the form of payment (bank draft, cashier's check, etc.).

When the buyer has agreed to get a loan from a third-party lender as part of the price, this loan must be approved before the closing can take place. Appraisals, credit reports, income verifications, surveys, and other items are to be processed by the mortgagee. Thus, allow some time between the date a purchase agreement is signed and the date of closing. Thirty days is usual, but the length of time will also depend on your area and how well the mortgage market and local attorneys are performing. If the seller is financing, the closing should take place in less time. Again, an experienced real estate professional will be able to help you identify and gather all necessary documents (e.g., 12 months paid-up hazard insurance policy as required by the mortgagee) before closing.

BUYING THE NEXT PROPERTY YOURSELF

The FSBO (''fiz-bo,'' for sale by owner) may be a good starting place for your next unit. The prospects suitable for your portfolio can sometimes be found merely by using the telephone. Look in the real estate section of newspapers, at signs in front of dwellings, and in the legal section of newspapers giving public notices of court-ordered sales (foreclosures, divorces, estates, etc.); get information from friends and acquaintances who know of a house being put on the market by an owner needing a quick sale. There is no question that an investor has a much better chance of getting a lower price on the house if he or she negotiates directly with the seller, cutting the broker's selling commission from the final price. Under these circumstances, though, do not expect any professional help from a salesperson.

Another good source of information about suitable properties is mortgage lenders. A good working relationship with the loan officers of a savings and loan will not only help you in financing properties, they sometimes know which homeowners are falling behind in monthly payments and want to sell before foreclosure proceedings begin. If you are a responsible businessperson buying and renting houses, these bankers may be able to help all parties concerned by carefully letting you know about the availability of such properties. Knowing a person who works in a private mortgage insurance company can be even better because he or she will come into contact with even more potential foreclosures.

As soon as you find a FSBO that is interesting to you, give the owner a call. You want to know the asking price, approximate square footage, number of rooms, age and general condition of the house, and any financial inducements offered by the seller. If the information sounds reasonable, then make an appointment to inspect the house and have a talk with the owner.

Be most objective and critical during this first visit. Do not attempt to impress the owner with your knowledge of real estate or with your position as an investor. In fact, it will be better not to reveal your intent. The first visit has two purposes, (1) to see whether or not this house can qualify as an unit in your portfolio; and (2) to lay the foundation for a working relationship with the owner. A record-keeping system similar to the one used for the first house should be employed for this one too. On this appointment do not point out to the owner or discuss with him any of the features you have noticed. You are only here to collect information for the purpose of comparing it with other alternatives. Should you decide to make an offer, however, you will have all the necessary particulars for negotiation purposes in you records.

While inspecting the house talk with the owner. Find out as much as you can about his or her situation. Feel free to talk about any outside interest he or she may have, but be sure to ask questions about the neighborhood, average utility bills, special extras of the house, age of the carpet and appliances, what will and will not remain in the house, and traffic patterns. Find out as much has you can about his or her likes and dislikes, but do not ask trivial, provocative questions, such as ''why did you choose this color carpet?'' Keep the conversation light and easy.

Make a special point of asking why the house is on the market and how long it has been for sale. If you are asked questions, be as honest and open as the situation allows. Avoid any controversial or argumentative conversations. If you like this property, you are going to return. The last thing you should do is reconfirm the asking price, ask about the mortgage balance and whether it is assumable.

Do your homework: Analyze this property using all the knowledge and information you have collected. Make arrangements with the owner to have estimates made of the cost of needed repairs. Check for any liens against the property, and for other deed restrictions or encumbrances. State law requires that all of this information be in the county courthouse. Depending on the state in which the investor resides, the office that keeps these records is known as the: County Clerk's Office, Circuit Clerk's Office, County Recorder's Office, County Registrar's Office, or the Bureau of Conveyances.

When the analysis is about finished, drive by the property again to see whether you have overlooked some feature, such as the drainage; is this property in a flood plain; are mud slides likely in rainy weather? Later on, find out if the water system, including sewer, freezes in very cold weather. As you go about investigating the property, keep your eyes open for any leads to something you should know but have overlooked.

Know the amount due on the mortgage or mortgages from your conversation with the seller. Find out whether he or she is in arrears on monthly payments, and if so by how much. (Get this information directly from the mortgagee; it is shown as a recorded lien in public documents. You may need a written statement from the seller to the mortgagee requesting exact information be sent to you.) If the owner has had work of any kind done on this property within the past few months, check with the company that did the work. If the bills were not paid, there may not have been time enough for a lien to be recorded. If there are outstanding debts, be prepared to discuss this with the owner during purchase negotiations, not before. When you begin to negotiate, you must know more about this property than its owner does.

During the negotiations, tactfully remind the owner of all the problems the property has. The yard needs work, the house needs paint, doors need to be replaced; the property is located on a busy street, is too far from convenient shopping, is too close to an elementary school; the house four doors down sold for $5,000 less than the asking price; the house does not quite fit your criteria, etc. The idea is that after considering all angles, you will buy the house at what it is worth *to you*. Always keep in mind that you are not in a hurry, the seller is.

EXAMPLE OF NEGOTIATING: You decide to make an offer for your second unit, a house owned by a retiree and his wife. They want to sell in order to move closer to their children. Reluctant to deal through a realtor, they have decided to sell their home themselves. They bought this as a new house directly from the builder

four years ago. It was financed under the GI bill with no down payment. The couple contracted to pay $55,000 with a 30-year mortgage
at 14 percent. Now, they are asking $75,000, and have had the house
on the market for over four months. These people do not fit our
description of motivated sellers, but you are quite interested in the
home.

The house has three bedrooms, two baths, a living room, dining
room, and a family room; the overall living space is approximately
1,520 square feet. There are five good-sized closets and a two-car
garage with electric door opener. There was a recent grease fire in
the kitchen. As a result, one wall needs repairing, the ceiling must
be painted and the stove replaced. The inexpensive carpets show
some wear. The exterior is a brick veneer over a wooden frame. The
roof is in good condition, but the interior walls and exterior trim
need painting. Both front and back yards are small, are covered with
tall grass, and have a few neatly trimmed shrubs. There are two restrictions on the deed, one is a city easement for sidewalks and
underground utility lines, the other a restriction on the size and type
of house that can be constructed in this neighborhood.

You have already noted all the problems of the house and discussed them with the owners; by now they probably are not overly
anxious to hear from you.

After doing a little figuring, you should prepare a purchase agreement, ready for the owner's signature, offering not more than
$62,500. (We will discuss pricing in Chapter 4.) The balance on the
$55,000 mortgage is about $54,400, with monthly payments of
$565.74 covering principal and interest. Add to this amount another
$100 for taxes and insurance and this leaves only a little room for
a reasonable income from rent. You plan to put down $500 plus clos-
ing costs (not more than $600).

The offer will be $58,500. After the purchase agreement is ready,
make an appointment to take it to the seller. Following the exchange
of a few friendly words, hand the contract over and excuse yourself
with a reasonable explanation for leaving. Just before you go, call
attention to the 24-hour time limit allowed for a decision.

When you call the next day, expect any kind of reception. The
owner may be angry and say something like, ''The price is too low
and we don't want to discuss it any further.'' Tell them you are sorry

that they are displeased, but if at a later time they would like an explanation of how you arrived at the price, you would be quite happy to discuss it with them. Wish them success in finding a buyer along with your farewell.

Unless you hear from them again within 14 days, drop this house from your list. Should the seller call back and appear ready to talk, prepare a short summary of the financial aspects of the home before you make another visit:

Payoff On Mortgage: $54,361.00
(Consider it your lucky break if the owner thought his equity was more than $639 after paying on the house for four years.) You obtained the payoff figure from the mortgagee.

Asking Price too High: Should be $70,000.00
Explain that the price of any real estate is the price agreed on between the seller and a willing, ready, and able buyer. Also add that when property is appraised for sale by a broker, the price quoted is often $5,000 higher than the broker expects to get, but gives some negotiating room, and also helps the broker to out bid other agencies for the listing. State that $70,000 is a relatively high price even if the home were sold through a broker. When sold by the owner, with no sales commission, the price should be lower by $4,200 or less.

Broker's commission: (5%–10%; here 6%) $4,200.00
This is the amount they would pay the agency to sell their house if they could get $70,000 for it.

Closing costs and points: Seller pays about $2,700.00
Show the purchase agreement containing your offer with the closing costs and points filled in. Make sure that you have marked in a little more than $2,700 for the seller.

Additional terms and conditions $4,600.00
Explain that you have added what any reasonable buyer would expect. For $70,000 anyone could buy a new house comparable to this one. Therefore, you, the buyer, have asked the owner to repaint the interior walls and exterior trim with colors and quality of paints that you select, and replace all the carpets with quality, color, and grade of padding of your choosing. The total deductions from the base price is $11,500, leaving a balance of $58,500, which is the amount of your offer, taking the property as is.

The seller may appear confused at this point. Explain to him that under the terms of your offer he is not responsible for closing costs and points, all added terms and conditions are eliminated, and there are no commissions for the seller to pay. Mark these items off the contract and add, "All closing costs paid by buyer," and initial each item you have cancelled.

Then you say something in the order of, "Let's take a look where all this leaves you." Explain that after closing, your proceeds will be $4,139. If the seller does not agree, then change your offer to $59,361 leaving the seller with a total of $5,000 after the closing. Be sure not to change the offer too quickly or the seller may get suspicious of some wrongdoing.

Also, inform him that you will assume the mortgage on this house, relieving him of this Veterans Administrations obligation and thereby freeing him to purchase another dwelling under the GI Bill with no required down payment. In other words, he and his wife have enough money to relocate and buy another home without touching any of their savings. You should also point out that if you had made an offer of $70,000 buying through a broker, you would have added in all these other costs, making their net return around $5,000, maybe less. (Because you are assuming his loan, closing costs are kept low and there are no points.)

Discuss any questions they may have, stressing the fact that they have accumulated only $639 in equity over four years, and that this little investment has resulted in $5,000. In addition, you will allow them to continue living here on a month-by-month rental basis, for up to four months (or whatever), paying the current monthly PITI payment as rent. Now is the time to suggest they "OK" the contract, but do not get pushy. If they want to think about it overnight, that will be fine. Be prepared to make a counter offer.

The fundamentals in the step-by-step procedure are:
1. Find out as much about the property as you can in the first telephone call.
2. Find out as much as you can about the owner's situation and why this house is on the market.
3. Find out about the condition of the house and lot, including costs of needed repairs and improvements.
4. Find out everything there is on the mortgages.
5. Know all there is to know about the deed restrictions such as liens, easements, eminent domain, encumbrances, encroach-

ments, and adverse possession. Also know the terms: escheat, fee simple, homestead protection laws, cloud on the title, and quitclaim deed. (See Glossary.)

6. Make your offer to purchase in the form of a contract, completed and signed by you.

7. During the negotiating session(s), make all of your points in favor of the seller; if you suggest any changes, make them in favor of the seller.

8. Do not prolong the negotiating session or the time for negotiations. As soon as you have finished explaining the terms of the contract, offer it to the seller to sign. If he or she does not sign and does not request a short delay in signing, pick up the contract, informing him or her that this offer is being withdrawn, but if they wish to pursue it later, to give you a call.

Chapter
Three

CASH FLOW AND SALES ANALYSIS

Whenever a real estate investment is being considered, a financial feasibility analysis must be prepared. Whether the potential property is a large multi-use development or a small condominium, an analysis of future costs and benefits will aid in the decision-making process and is required by most lenders. Because these computations are usually performed using a computer, many reports are generated on a ''pro forma'' (what if) basis in that any variable can be easily changed to reflect different outcomes, such as pessimistic, most likely to occur, and optimistic. In addition, each year of proposed ownership should be considered to reflect economic changes on an annual basis.

The objective of working through a financial feasibility analysis is to test the overall economics of a deal. It is set up for each property over a proposed period of ownership, which, under normal circumstances, is anywhere from three to eight years. A cash-flow analysis and sales analysis are two important summaries in a financial feasibility study. The input for the two summaries consists of expected revenues and expenses and other variables which can be adjusted according to an individual's perception of future economic events. Afterward, the present value of both the annual cash flows from operation and eventual sales proceeds are combined and compared to the total initial investment. The figures derived from this comparison will give a "buy" or "not buy" recommendation. Other summaries, such as a mortgage data report, depreciation report, property summary report, and total debt-service summary, may also be presented in a financial feasibility analysis. Prospective lenders or investors or both are interested in evaluating the reasonableness of the summaries for obvious purposes. Once a project is under way, however, the analysis will serve as a guideline, budget, and/or record-keeping device in tracking the financial status of an investment (by simply incorporating actual amounts into the computation as the amounts become known).

CASH-FLOW ANALYSIS

Most examinations of a real estate investment will include a cash-flow analysis. This is a hypothetical summary showing expected revenues, expenses, tax benefits, and net cash flow for any given period of time (usually annually). There are many variations, usually depending on the sum involved. The larger the amount, the more sophisticated and detailed the procedure becomes. For our purposes—because we are not dealing in seven-figure amounts yet— a basic report will be quite satisfactory. Generally, however, all cash-flow analyses are presented in similar fashion.

The **cash flow from operations** formula is first used to compute net operating income (NOI), then taxable income or loss; once these two amounts are calculated, cash flow after taxes is derived as follows:

CASH-FLOW FORMULA

(1)		Gross Rental Income
(2)	LESS:	Vacancies and Credit Losses
(3)	LESS:	Operating Expenses
(4)	EQUALS:	Net Operating Income (NOI)
(5)	LESS:	Interest Deduction
(6)	LESS:	Depreciation Deduction
(7)	EQUALS:	Taxable Income (Loss)

(8)		Net Operating Income (NOI)
(9)	LESS:	Debt Service
	EQUALS:	Cash Flow before Income Tax
(10)	ADD:	Tax Benefit (or LESS: Additional Tax Paid)
(11)	EQUALS:	Cash Flow after Income Tax

(1) Gross rental income is found by multiplying the expected monthly rent by 12 months. Generally, the current rent or fair market rental for comparable property in the area is used. Inquiring about comparable properties in the neighborhood or checking advertisements are usually good sources for estimating this figure.

(2) Vacancies and credit losses are a percentage of gross rental income. The percentage usually used for real estate offerings is 5 percent, however, 10–20 percent may be more accurate depending upon the type of property and its location. Other investors, real estate consultants, or real estate brokers who know the area are good sources for determining the proper percentage on a particular property. Some computations label the difference between gross operating income and vacancy/credit losses *gross possible income* (GPI).

(3) Operating expenses are all cash expenses paid excluding any portion of the mortgage payment (i.e., interest and depreciation—a noncash expense—are not included). Operating expenses include building maintenance, ground maintenance, utilities, repairs, taxes, insurance, and management costs. The seller, other investors, and/or real estate brokers may provide estimates of these costs. Some computations label the balance of gross operating income less vacancy/credit losses and operating expenses *gross effective income* (GEI).

(4) Net operating income (NOI) is an amount frequently mentioned in real estate investment offerings and is the starting figure in computing cash flow before income tax. It is sometimes used in comparing the "economics" of different properties in that all tax deductions are not used in its computation—only vacancy/credit losses and operating expenses are included.

(5) Interest deduction is the amount allowable for income tax purposes. Taxpayers who have a great number of investment interest deductions in one tax year may find that the amount they can deduct is limited. The advice of an accountant or other tax expert is helpful here.

(6) Depreciation deduction is the amount of depreciation allowable for income tax purposes. The day the property was "placed in service" is important in determining which depreciation schedule can be used. We will use a 27.5-year straight-line depreciation in our examples, but a tax consultant will know whether another method or term has become available. Note that only the amount of basis that is allocated to a building is depreciable. The amount allocated to land is not depreciable. (Basis is discussed in Chapter 5.) The allocation is made in terms of the ratio of respective fair market values at the time of acquisition as derived by professional appraisals or by the local tax assessor's office.

(7) The amount of taxable income (or loss) is necessary for determining the effect of taxes on cash flow. If there is a deductible loss, then cash flow will increase by the amount of benefit received (i.e., the amount of taxes saved). If there is taxable income, then cash flow will decrease by the amount of taxes paid.

(8) NOI is the first computation used for determining cash flow. As noted previously, interest and depreciation expenses are not included in its computation. Thus, NOI consists of only cash rental revenues (net of vacancy/credit losses) and cash operating expenses. (Recall that interest is not an operating expense and depreciation is a noncash expense.)

(9) Debt service is the total amount of the mortgage payment. It includes both interest and principal. Because debt service is an outflow of cash, and interest—a nonoperating cash expense—is not included in NOI, the entire mortgage payment must be subtracted from net operating income in order to arrive at cash flow before the effects of income taxes. (The payment of principal on a loan is never classified as an expense, but it is an outflow of cash that reduces a liability.)

(10) The tax benefit is the amount of money saved by creating a

deductible loss. It is found by multiplying the deductible loss by your marginal tax rate. Thus, an investor who has a marginal tax rate of 30 percent and incurs a $10,000 deductible *loss* will save $3,000 (30 percent × $10,000) in taxes paid: In effect, net cash flow increases by $3,000. On the other hand, if revenues were to exceed all deductions and, say, taxable *income* was $12,000 (marginal tax rate is still 30 percent), then $3,600 would have to be paid in taxes: Cash flow decreases by $3,600. In either case, the taxable loss or income is multiplied by the marginal tax rate to arrive at the benefit or additional tax.

(11) Cash flow after income tax shows the projected outcome of a prospective rental property's operation for one period.

EXAMPLE OF CASH-FLOW ANALYSIS   Suppose you are in a 28 percent marginal tax bracket and you are analyzing a rental house that is listed for $125,000. The allocated basis for the structure is $100,000 and for the land is $25,000. Monthly rent is $725; all operating expenses are currently $1,600 per year. After a 20 percent down payment is made, the amount borrowed would be $100,000, which would involve a monthly mortgage payment (principal and interest) of $877.58 on a loan carrying 10 percent interest for 30 years. The vacancy/credit loss rate for the area is 10 percent. The first 12-month cash flow summary is as follows (assuming all of the taxable loss is deductible):

	Gross rental income	$ 8,700
Less:	Vacancies/credit losses	− 870
Less:	Operating Expenses	− 1,600
	Net Operating Income	6,230
Less:	Interest Deduction	− 10,000*
Less:	Depreciation	− 3,636**
	Taxable loss	$ −7,406
	Net Operating Income	$ 6,230
Less:	Debt service	− 10,531
	Cash flow before income tax	− 4,301
Add:	Tax benefit	+ 2,074***
	Cash flow after taxes	$ −2,227

  *$100,000 loan balance × 10% interest.
 **$100,000 basis/27.5 years.
*** −$7,406 taxable loss × 28% tax rate.

SALES ANALYSIS

From the preceding computation alone, you probably are not interested in the property unless its future selling price is worthy of a negative cash flow. In the parlance of real estate investing, you would be "betting on the come" should you decide to purchase the property as presented above. That is, you are anticipating higher future NOIs and a higher property value on the selling date to obtain the required profit. Inflation will certainly enhance your scenario. A sales analysis using your variables will help determine the property's feasibility as an investment. The sales analysis formula is as follows:

Sales Analysis Formula

(1)		Selling Price
(2)	LESS:	Selling Expenses
(3)	LESS:	Mortgage Balance
	EQUALS:	Proceeds before Income Tax
(4)	LESS:	Additional Income Tax Due
(5)	EQUALS:	Net Sales Proceeds

---

(1) The selling price is found by estimating the amount of annual increase in value you expect the property to experience. Recent value increases for the last two years should be considered, but the expectation of an area's growth and development are the most important factors to weigh. Real estate brokers and consultants are two good sources to check. Once a reasonable annual growth rate is found, it should be compounded by the formula $(1 + i)^n$ (where i = annual growth rate, and n = number of years of ownership) and then multiplied by the purchase price to derive the expected selling price.

(2) Selling expenses are amounts paid for real estate commissions, title charges, tax stamps, attorney's fees, surveys, appraisals, points, and any other similar costs borne by the seller. A general figure to use here is 10 percent of the selling price.

(3) The mortgage balance is the amount needed to pay off the loan at the time the property is sold. It must be subtracted from the gross sales proceeds to find the amount available to the investor after the sale.

(4) Additional income taxes may be incurred as a result of the sale and should be included in the computation. The amount of tax liability is virtually always uncertain in that tax rates and/or capital gain taxation may change by the time the property is sold. Nevertheless, it is better to be conservative by consistently applying some tax rate, such as 28 percent, to all property evaluations. (Most of our examples and problems use 28 percent.) The method of computing taxable gain on sale is selling price less adjusted basis. (Generally, the adjusted basis is equal to a property's original cost plus any capitalized improvements less depreciation.)

(5) Net sales proceeds are the amount of money you expect to receive at the close of the sale. Because the sum will be received at a certain time in the future, it must be discounted by present value factors and compared to your initial investment, as shown in the present value of all cash flows summary.

EXAMPLE OF SALES ANALYSIS Suppose property values in the area are projected to increase by an average of 16 percent over the next 12 months. Being a little conservative, you chose 15 percent so that the expected selling price in one year would be $143,750 [$125,000 $\times$ (1 + .15)^1]. The mortgage balance would be approximately $99,469 [$100,000 loan − (12 $\times$ $877.58 total debt service − $10,000 interest)].

	Selling Price	$143,750
Less:	Selling Expenses	− 14,375
Less:	Mortgage Balance	− 99,469
	Proceeds before Tax	$ 29,906
Less:	Additional Tax	− 6,268*
	Net Sales Proceeds	$ 23,638

*($143,750 sales price − $121,364 basis) $\times$ 28% tax rate.
(Basis is $125,000 original basis − $3,636 depreciation.)

PRESENT VALUE OF ALL CASH FLOWS

This is merely a summary of the present value of aftertax cash flows from operations throughout the ownership period plus the sales proceeds. The present value of all cash flows is as follows:

Present Value of All Cash Flows

(1)		Present Value of Aftertax Cash Flows
(2)	ADD:	Present Value of Net Sales Proceeds
	EQUALS:	Total Present Value of Investment
(3)	COMPARED TO:	Cost of Investment

---

(1) The present value of aftertax cash flows is calculated by multiplying a present value factor times the aftertax cash flow for each year shown in the analysis. The rate of interest to be used in computing the present value factor is the lowest rate that an investor expects to earn from investing in this particular property. Given other alternatives and the amount of risk involved, the rate should obviously be higher than those of safer, more predictable investments. One reasonable investment philosophy is to use 150 percent of the prevailing prime rate. For the examples and problems in this chapter, however, we will use 15 percent as the required rate of return for residential real estate investing.

   The formula for a present value factor is $1/(1 + i)^n$. Because we have arbitrarily chosen 15 percent, the factor for one year is .8695652 $[1/(1.15)^1]$.

(2) The present value of net sales proceeds is also calculated by multiplying a present value factor times the amount of money expected to be received. The rate of interest used in computing the present value of aftertax cash flows is also used here. Note that a property to be held for five years would have five different present value factors in computing the sum of aftertax cash flows (one for each year), but only one factor would be used for net sales proceeds (the factor for the fifth year).

(3) Given the variables prescribed by you, the comparison of the present value of the investment to its purchase price reveals the buy or not buy result. If the present value of the investment equals or exceeds your cost and all other aspects appear favorable, then buy it: The proposed investment meets your criteria. Should the present value of the investment be less than the purchase price, then strictly from a financial viewpoint, this investment is not for you.

EXAMPLE OF PRESENT VALUE OF ALL CASH FLOWS We will use the data from the two previous summaries in a present value calculation. Our computation is simplified because we only show a proposed ownership period of one year.

Present Value of Aftertax Cash Flow	$-1,937*
Present Value of Net Sales Proceeds	20,555**
Total Present Value of Investment	$ 18,618
Cost of Investment	$ 25,000

*($-2,227 × .8695652)
**($23,638 × .8695652)

It is now quite obvious that the proposed investment in its current position is not a plausible alternative for your portfolio.

PROBLEM II – Feasibility Analysis

You are looking at a house that sells for $140,000. The owner is willing to finance 90 percent at an interest rate of 10 percent for 30 years, which yields a monthly payment of $1,105.74 ($1,106 rounded). An independent professional appraisal shows the building to be worth $125,000 and the land $25,000. Monthly operating expenses are expected to be $125, and rent is set at $1,200 per month. Operating expenses are expected to rise at an annual rate of 10 percent, while monthly rentals will increase by an annual rate of 3 percent.

Vacancy and credit losses are 10 percent in the area. Assume you are in a 28 percent marginal tax bracket, 27.5-year straight-line depreciation is used, all losses are deductible, values are reasonably projected to rise at a rate of 7 percent per year, and your expected rate of return is 25 percent. Is this investment financially feasible? Show a proposed ownership period of three full years with selling expenses of 5 percent on future sale.

(The annual interest deduction and mortgage balance at the end of year 3 as shown in the answer will be slightly different because of monthly—i.e., regular—amortization rather than yearly amortization. Also, first-year depreciation, third-year depreciation, and additional tax paid on sale will be slightly different because of the mid-month convention rules, which are discussed in Chapter 5.)

Chapter
Four

FINANCIAL ANALYSIS

Once cash flow and sales proceeds for a given property have been analyzed, the investor needs a way of evaluating and comparing these figures for various properties. The following methods are common techniques of determining whether the return (yield) from a given investment is sufficient to warrant the outlay.

INTERNAL RATE OF RETURN (IRR)

The internal rate of return provides a computation that can be used to compare the yields from alternative investments such as bonds, stocks, and commodities. It has therefore become one of the most popular measures in real estate investing and is widely used in real estate investment literature as well as in promotional materials. Because of the internal rate of return's popularity, it is given more emphasis than other financial analysis techniques.

In general, IRR is a rate at which the present value of all cash flows exactly equals the initial investment. Note that for the feasibility analysis problem at the end of Chapter 3, the internal rate of return would equal exactly 26.784 percent if the initial out-of-pocket investment was $14,618.

Here is another way to visualize what IRR is. Suppose instead of making a proposed real estate investment, we put money into, say, bonds with a fixed rate of return. The question is: What would the bonds have to earn (neglecting income taxes for the moment) to make them as attractive an investment as a real estate opportunity? That rate is the internal rate of return.

For bonds and other similar investments, then, IRR is equivalent to the "yield to maturity" or "market rate of interest." For example, suppose you were offered $15,000 in exactly four years for investing $10,000 today in 15 zero coupon bonds (compounded annually). What would your internal rate of return be before income taxes? (Answer: 10.67%.)

In real estate the same principle applies: We project the future value of all cash flows, discount them at an "acceptable" rate using present value factors, and compare the sum of discounted cash flows (i.e., present value of net cash flows) with the initial investment. When both figures are equal, the "acceptable" rate *is* the internal rate of return: net present value (NPV = 0). However, when the discounted sum is greater than the initial investment (NPV > 0), as shown in the answer to the feasibility problem at the end of Chapter 3 (NPV = $618), then the projected internal rate of return is greater than the acceptable rate; the project appears to be financially favorable.

All internal rate of return problems must be done by trial and error. Initially, you must arbitrarily pick an IRR and work through the following formula:

$$\text{INITIAL INVESTMENT} = \frac{\text{Expected Cash Flow, Year 1}}{(1+\text{IRR})^1} + \frac{\text{Expected Cash Flow, Year 2}}{(1+\text{IRR})^2} + \ldots \frac{\text{Expected Cash Flow, Year } n}{(1+\text{IRR})^n}$$

There are many programmable calculators and computer programs that can calculate IRR very quickly. If you do not have access to one, you can still work through the following problems with an ordinary calculator.

To illustrate internal rate of return, suppose you were to invest $200,000 today and are to receive $22,000 per year for the next two years. In addition, at the end of year 2 you are to receive $232,000. What is this investment's IRR? The formula is shown below:

$$\$200{,}000 \; = \; \frac{\$22{,}000}{(1+\text{IRR})^1} \; + \; \frac{\$22{,}000}{(1+\text{IRR})^2} \; + \; \frac{\$232{,}000}{(1+\text{IRR})^2}$$

Stated another way:

$$\$200{,}000 \; = \; (\$22{,}000)\,\frac{1}{(1+\text{IRR})^1} \; + \; (\$22{,}000)\,\frac{1}{(1+\text{IRR})^2}$$

$$+ \; (\$232{,}000)\,\frac{1}{(1+\text{IRR})^2}$$

Where $\dfrac{1}{(1+\text{IRR})^n}$ computes a present value factor.

In order to compute IRR, we must arbitrarily choose a rate of return and work through the computation to see how close we can come to $200,000. Initially, we chose 12 percent and computed present value factors, which were taken from the formula above:

Present Value Factors @ 12 %

$$\text{YEAR 1} \; = \; \frac{1}{(1+.12)^1} \; = \; .8928571$$

$$\text{YEAR 2} \; = \; \frac{1}{(1+.12)^2} \; = \; .7971938$$

	PV FACTOR @12%		EXPECTED CASH FLOW		PV CASH FLOW
YR 1	.8928571	×	$22,000	=	$ 19,643
YR 2	.7971938	×	$22,000	=	17,538
YR 2	.7971938	×	$232,000	=	184,948
	TOTAL PV OF CASH FLOWS @ 12%				$222,130

Because the total PV of cash flows is greater than our initial investment, the IRR must be greater than 12 percent. So, we chose 18 percent and worked through the computation again:

Present Value Factors @ 18%

$$\text{Year 1} = \frac{1}{(1+.18)^1} = .8474576$$

$$\text{Year 2} = \frac{1}{(1+.18)^2} = .7181844$$

	PV FACTOR @ 18%		EXPECTED CASH FLOW		PV CASH FLOW
YR 1	.8474576	×	$22,000	=	$ 18,644
YR 2	.7181844	×	$22,000	=	15,800
YR 2	.7181844	×	$232,000	=	166,619
	TOTAL PV OF CASH FLOWS @ 18%				$201,062

We are close enough to $200,000 to determine that the IRR is just over 18 percent for this particular investment. With enough attempts, we could get extremely close to the actual figure. However, the difference of .003284 is hardly worth the effort to compute unreasonably accurate percentages for these investments.

PROBLEM III — INTERNAL RATE OF RETURN
(uneven cash flows)

You invested $120,000 in rental property and expect to receive net cash flow of $5,000 in year 1, $7,500 in year 2, and $10,000 in year 3. Also in the third year, you plan to sell the investment and net $175,000. What is the internal rate of return for this venture?

Answer:

Just under 19 percent as determined as follows:

PV @ 19%

YR 1	.8403361	× $5,000	=	$ 4,202
YR 2	.7061648	× $7,500	=	5,296
YR 3	.5934158	× $10,000	=	5,934
YR 3	.5934158	× $175,000	=	103,848

Total PV of Cash flows @ 19% $119,280

ADJUSTED INTERNAL RATE OF RETURN (AFTERTAX RATE)
Most investment yields (IRR calculations) are stated as beforetax percentages that assume compounding of interest. The yield to maturity on the zero coupon bond computed at the beginning of the chapter, for example, was a before-income-tax percentage that took compounding into consideration. In other words, if you were to invest $10,000 in a savings account that compounded interest annually at 10.67 percent, you would have $15,000 at the end of four years if there were no income taxes to be paid during the four-year period. Obviously, an aftertax yield for the savings account would decrease depending on an individual's marginal tax bracket.

Note that in our computation of cash flow (Chapter 3, p. 56) we took income taxes into consideration and ended up with an *aftertax cash flow* figure for each year of ownership. We also considered the effect of income tax on the sale of the property. If we calculate IRR in this manner, we will show an aftertax yield. The rate of return on alternative investments must be adjusted by multiplying the complement of the marginal tax rate (1 − marginal tax rate) by the before-tax percentage on alternative investments. For example, assume that a taxpayer, who is in the 15 percent tax bracket, is interested in the 10.67 percent savings account. His aftertax yield will be only 9.07 percent [(1−.15) × 10.67%] should he invest in the savings account.

REINVESTMENT AND IRR   Another important consideration here is that the internal rate of return not only provides for compounding, but does so at a constant rate. Stated another way, all IRR computations thus far have assumed that the net cash proceeds (rentals) received during the years of ownership were *reinvested* at the same rate calculated for the internal rate of return. Reinvestment is the primary characteristic of compounding.

In the previous example where you invested $200,000 and were to receive $22,000 per year for two years, the IRR was just over 18 percent. Thus, as you received the $22,000 in year 1, the IRR computation took into consideration that you immediately reinvested the proceeds in another investment yielding 18 percent rather than using the cash for other purposes or reinvesting it in an investment yielding a different rate. In most cases, however, cash proceeds are rarely reinvested in a vehicle yielding the same rate as the calculated IRR. When reinvestment does occur, it is usually in a different investment which provides a lower rate of return. Reinvestment differentials are particularly important for investors primarily concerned with analyzing income-producing properties.

In adjusting the internal rate of return computation for a reinvestment differential, we must first determine the "future value" of all cash flows in accordance with an investor's reinvestment rate of return, total the adjusted cash flows, and then find the rate for a future value factor that can be multiplied by the cost of the investment to equal the sum of future cash flows—again, by trial and error. The formula for future value is as follows:

$$\text{Amount to be Compounded} \times (1+i)^n$$

where i = an investor's reinvestment rate, and n = the number of periods a sum of money is to be compounding. Rentals to be received throughout the year are considered to be received at year end for purposes of this computation.

For example, assume you were to purchase a single-family residence for $80,000 (equity) and were able to net $5,000, $7,500, $8,000, and $8,500 per year over the next four years, respectively. At the end of four years, you plan to net $110,000 after selling the property. The rate of interest at which you will reinvest the cash proceeds received from the rentals (the reinvestment rate) is 10 percent. The internal rate of return will be computed this manner:

YR 1	YR 2	YR 3	FUTURE VALUE @ YR 4
$5000 \times (1.10)^3$			$ 6,655
	$7500 \times (1.10)^2$		9,075
		$8000 \times (1.10)^1$...	8,800
			8,500
Total FV of Net Cash Rentals			$ 33,030
Future Selling Price (Net)			+$110,000
Total FV of the Investment (YR 4)			$143,030
Total Investment Cost			$80,000

Now we must determine—through trial and error—at what aftertax rate an $80,000 investment will yield a return of approximately $143,030 in four years using the formula for future value. We computed the future value of $80,000 using three different rates:

@ 12%	@ 15%	@ 15.5%
$(1.12)^4 = 1.5735$	$(1.15)^4 = 1.7490$	$(1.15.5)^4 = 1.7796$
$1.5735 \times 80,000$	$1.7490 \times 80,000$	$1.7796 \times 80,000$
$= 125,880$	$= 139,920$	$= 142,368$

Thus, the internal rate of return for the investment, adjusted for a different reinvestment rate, is slightly above 15.5 percent.

Even if an investor does not chose to reinvest the rentals, the reinvestment rate should still be used in the computation for purposes of comparison. If profits are not reinvested, the reinvestment rate used would be the aftertax rate that an investor could receive on a low-risk alternative investment.

LEVERAGE AND IRR   Thus far in this chapter we have only considered cases in which an investor purchases property without using leverage. Whenever a property purchase is financed using leverage and the property increases in value, the IRR will be enhanced, as illustrated in the following problem:

You purchased a house for $150,000 by putting 10 percent down ($15,000) and financing the balance. Your expected net cash flows over the next five years are as follows: $600, $650, $700, $600, and $750. Also, in the fifth year, the property is to be sold for $190,000 (4.84 percent annual increase in value), which will provide net cash proceeds of approximately $30,000. Assuming your reinvestment rate is the same as the IRR (this is not a significant aspect here because the cash flows are relatively small), what is your internal rate of return for investing in this project?

After trying a few rates, 18 percent was found to be the closest one:

	PV FACTOR @ 18%		EXPECTED CASH FLOW		PV CASH FLOW
YR 1	.8474576	×	$600	=	$ 508
YR 2	.7181844	×	$650	=	467
YR 3	.6086309	×	$700	=	426
YR 4	.5157889	×	$600	=	309
YR 5	.4371092	×	$750	=	328
YR 5	.4371092	×	$30,000	=	13,113
	Total PV of All Cash Flows @ 18%				$15,151

Notice the house only experienced a 4.84 percent increase in value over the four-year period, yet the internal rate of return on your cash investment is slightly below 18 percent—primarily because of leveraging.

RATE OF RETURN ON TOTAL CAPITAL (ROR)

The rate of return on total capital is also widely used in evaluating real estate investments. It measures the productivity of the total cost of an investment (i.e., debt and equity) over a *one-year period*. Internal rate of return measures the productivity of an equity investment over the entire ownership period. The ROR presents the relationship between net operating income and the total cost of the project:

$$ROR = \frac{\text{Net Operating Income (NOI)}}{\text{Total Capital}}$$

In the feasibility analysis problem at the end of Chapter 3, you analyzed a rental house costing $140,000 for which the net operating income was projected to be $11,699 in the second year. Thus, the rate of return on total capital for that project during the second year would be 8.36 percent (11,699/140,000). The ROR reports percentages *before* income taxes.

RATE OF RETURN ON EQUITY (ROE)

The rate of return on equity percentage is probably the most frequently used ratio in analyzing *income-producing* real estate investments. It is similar to rate of return on total capital, but only takes into account net cash flow and equity investment. ROE measures the ability of an equity investment to generate cash flow over a one-year period and typically changes each year:

$$ROE = \frac{\text{Net Cash Flow}}{\text{Equity}}$$

In the leverage and IRR example on page 74, the cash flow after income taxes for the first year was $600, and for the second year was $650. The amount of equity invested was $15,000. The rate of return on equity for the first year is 4 percent (600/15,000), and for the second year, 4.33 percent (650/15,000).

Remember that these percentages are net of income tax (i.e., showing an aftertax yield). Be aware that some ROE computations, however, will substitute *cash flow before income taxes* instead of net cash flow in the numerator and thereby present a beforetax yield, which would make the figure higher.

MAXIMUM EQUITY INVESTMENT

A question that many real estate investors consistently face is ''how much equity is 'too much' equity?'' Obviously, the lowest amount invested (not including zero) will yield the best rate of return on equity if cash flow is relatively stable and property values increase. Although ''nothing down'' deals appear to be quite effective, they are extremely rare. Even when one arises, an investor will likely wind up making improvements to the property, incur closing costs, and pay for other similar costs to complete the purchase or ready the property for resale, which are all considered to be equity investment outlays.

To answer the question of ''how much is too much,'' two different approaches are presented here. A strategist whose main objective is income-producing property (value appreciation being a secondary objective) will use a simple ratio after determining expected annual average cash flow over the period of ownership and determining the rate of return on equity investment that he or she requires:

$$\text{Maximum Equity Investment} = \frac{\text{Expected Average Annual Net Cash Flow}}{\text{Required Rate of Return on Equity Investment (ROE)}}$$

$$\frac{1,500}{15\%} = 10,000$$

For example, assume you expect a property to yield an average annual net cash flow of $6,000 and your required rate of return on equity is 12 percent. The maximum amount of investment outlay would be $50,000 ($6,000/12%). Suppose you were dealing with a seller who needs immediate cash and is also willing to finance part of the selling price. His home, which is in great shape, is valued at $90,000, but he is in quite a hurry to sell. So, after determining the fair monthly rental value for the property ($875), the amount of cash *you* require per month ($475—includes vacancy/credit losses and tax benefits), and the residual cash flow for debt service, taxes, and insurance—$400 ($875 − $475), you decide to offer him $50,000 down and have him take back a second mortgage of $25,000 over 20 years at 10 percent. This will allow you to make a mortgage payment of just $241 per month, leaving $159 ($400 − $241) to cover operating expenses. If your seller thinks this is the best deal he can get, you will have purchased a rental house for a price that was determined using this simple formula. Notice that in this example, the total purchase price was not presented, only the terms of the deal.

The second approach uses internal rate of return, thereby taking into consideration the aftertax cash flow of both peroidically received rentals and eventual sales proceeds. The first step is to determine a required rate of return, and then compute the present value of all expected cash receipts, just as we did in Chapter 3. If there is a net present value (NPV—the excess of the sum of discounted cash flows over your initial investment) after you make the computation, then this figure will serve as a limit for the amount of immediate capital improvements you can make to the property and still achieve your required rate of return.

Recall the feasibility analysis problem at the end of Chapter 3, where our purchase price was $140,000, initial cash investment was $14,000 and the sum of discounted net cash flows was $14,618 (NPV = $618). This means that we can still make $618 of capital improvements or offer $618 more—if we have to in order to make the deal—and still maintain a 25 percent rate of return on invested capital.

As an example, assume an investor's expected ownership period is six years, net cash flow per year is $1,200, and he purchases a home for $100,000. He expects to get $32,500 on resale (after taxes), which is conceivable given a 5 percent annual increase in value and 90 percent leverage. Given the risks involved for the property, the investor's required rate of return is 25 percent, which provides a sum of discounted cash flows equal to about $12,050. In this case, he should pay no more equity than $12,050, if all other variables are reasonably close to actual amounts. But if he only puts up $10,000 (10 percent), then he will experience a rate of return greater than 25 percent.

GROSS RENT MULTIPLIER (GRM)

Some sellers and real estate agents will use a gross rent multiplier as a ''rule of thumb'' estimate of market values for residential properties. It is not an accurate measurement because income taxes, vacancies, credit losses, management fees, operating expenses, improvements, and property taxes are not considered in the computation:

$$\text{Gross Rent Multiplier} = \frac{\text{Property Value}}{\text{Gross Possible Income}}$$

$$\frac{27,000}{5,400} = 5.0 \qquad \text{smaller is better}$$

''Gross possible income'' is the total amount of rental income that a property can produce, which is computed by multiplying the property's monthly fair rental value times 12 months.

The gross rent multiplier computation, however, is useful for making a quick comparison of property values within a certain geographic area. Not only will the average GRM be different in different cities, but it can also vary between subdivisions within the same city or metropolitan area because of different property and rental values. You can get the GRMs for areas in which you intend to invest by asking real estate professionals or other investors who are knowledgeable about such matters. In addition, you should strongly consider making some GRM computations yourself once an area's property values and fair rentals are determined. This will give you a quick measure for ''ballpark'' valuations.

For example, suppose you were looking at a house in a nice subdivision where the fair rental per month would be $1,500. You know the average GRM for the area is 8.2. The property is listed for $160,000, but your rule of thumb value puts it around $147,600 [($1,500 × 12) × 8.2] for purposes of turning it into a rental home.

PROBLEM IV – FINANCIAL ANALYSIS

The following information was gathered and computed by researching a prospective rental residence:

Purchase price	$150,000
Estimated value increase per year	3%
Percentage financed	90%
Years to be held	6
Fair monthly rental	$1,400
Required rate of return	18%
Expected net sales proceeds	$33,160
Marginal tax rate	28%

Expected net cash flows:

YR1	$ 250
YR2	685
YR3	1,145
YR4	1,625
YR5	2,130
YR6	2,655
Net operating income—yr1	$12,720
Net operating income—yr6	$16,234

Answer each question individually from the data given above:

1. What is the internal rate of return for this investment? (Disregard reinvestment rate.)
2. What is the internal rate of return for this investment for an investor having a reinvestment rate of 6 percent? Would this computation be affected if cash flows per year were about $5,000 and expected net sales proceeds were only $8,000? Explain.

3. What is the rate of return on total capital (ROR) for the first year? (Assume no other capital expenditures were made.) What is the ROR in the sixth year?
4. What is the rate of return on equity (ROE) for the second year? (Assume no other capital expenditures were made.) What is the ROE in the fifth year?
5. What is the maximum equity investment for this project? (Use the net present value method.)
6. If the average GRM for the area is 7.9, is this house priced above or below normal? What if the GRM is 9.1, is the house priced about right?
7. If the value ($150,000) is appropriate for the area, is this a good investment?

Answers

1. Slightly below 20%:
   Present value of net cash flows @ 20% . . . .

$$PV\ FORMULA\ =\ \frac{1}{(1\ +\ IRR)^n}$$

where IRR = arbitrarily chosen internal rate of return

n = year

YR	PV FACTOR @ 20%		CASH FLOW		PV CASH FLOW
1.	.8333333	×	250	=	208
2.	.6944444	×	685	=	476
3.	.5787037	×	1,145	=	663
4.	.4822530	×	1,625	=	784
5.	.4018775	×	2,130	=	856
6.	.3348979	×	2,655	=	889
6.	.3348979	×	33,160	=	11,105

PV OF INVESTMENT @ 20%   14,981

2. Using the "reinvestment method," slightly below 19%:

YR1	YR2	YR3	YR4	YR5	=	YR6
250×1.06^5					=	335
	685×1.06^4				=	865
		1145×1.06^3			=	1,364
			1625×1.06^2		=	1,826
				2130×1.06	=	2,258
						2,655
						33,160

FUTURE VALUE OF ALL CASH PROCEEDS @ 6%   42,463

TOTAL EQUITY   15,000

FV @ 18%	**FV @ 19%**
$15000 \times (1.18)^6$	$15000 \times (1.19)^6$
= 40,493	= 42,596

If cash flows per year equaled $5,000 and sales proceeds were expected to be $8,000, there would be no significant difference in the outcome:

Adding the future value factors from above (PV of an annuity) =

$$(1.06)^5 + (1.06)^4 + (1.06)^3 + (1.06)^2 + (1.06) = 5.975319$$

YRS	CASH FLOW	FV FACTOR		AMOUNT STATED @ FV (6TH YR)
1–5	5,000	× 5.975319	=	29,877
6	5,000	—	=	5,000
6	8,000	—	=	8,000

TOTAL FV OF CASH FLOWS @ 6%   42,877

FV of 15,000 @ 19% (from above)   42,596

3. ROR yr1 =   8.5% (12,720/150,000)
    ROR yr6 = 10.8% (16,234/150,000)

4. ROE yr2 =   4.57% (685/15,000)
    ROE yr5 = 14.2% (2,130/15,000)

5. Maximum equity investment is $16,436.91:

YR	PV FACTOR @ 18%		CASH FLOW		DISCOUNTED CASH FLOW
1	.8474576	×	250	=	211.86
2	.7181844	×	685	=	491.96
3	.6086308	×	1,145	=	696.88
4	.5157888	×	1,625	=	838.16
5	.4371092	×	2,130	=	931.04
6	.3704315	×	2,655	=	983.50
6	.3704315	×	33,160	=	12,283.51

PRESENT VALUE OF INVESTMENT @ 18%   16,436.91

6. GRM @ 7.9 = 132,720 (house is priced too high)
   GRM @ 9.1 = 152,880 (house is priced about right)

7. Given the investor's required rate of return (18 percent) and assuming all assumptions are reasonable for the area (e.g., rate of value appreciation at 3 percent per year, $1,400 rental per month, 90 percent financing for 30 years, and net cash flow), then yes, this is an excellent investment provided the house meets all other requirements.

Chapter
Five

INCOME TAX CONSIDERATIONS

The tax consequences of every real estate transaction must be considered in light of your unique income tax situation. Adding to this complexity, tax laws and procedures are continually changing. Depending on the amounts involved and the impact a real estate transaction could have, you must decide whether you need the services of a tax consultant. Our advice: consult a tax advisor for all your real estate transactions.

Appropriate structuring of your investments can make a big difference, and you may not be aware of the tax consequences that even the slightest adjustment can make to your cash flow (e.g., form of business entity; active versus passive participation; method of depreciation; method of accounting; when to place in service; improvement versus ''expensing''; when and how to sell, exchange, or otherwise dispose of property). Be sure to seek the services of a tax advisor who is knowledgeable in the field of real estate. Not all accountants and attorneys are qualified to advise in this area.

CLASSIFICATION OF REAL ESTATE

For our purposes, real estate is property ''held for the production of income,'' a personal residence, or property held by a ''dealer.'' Each classification has different tax effects.

Generally, rental properties are considered to be real estate held for production of income. This distinction is important because under ordinary circumstances, depreciation can be taken; the properties qualify for a tax-free exchange, and if these properties are donated to a qualified charity, they may be valued at fair market value rather than at cost. In addition, necessary operating expenses as well as dispositions resulting in a loss will be deductible under appropriate conditions.

Property held as a personal residence cannot be fully depreciated and cannot always qualify for a tax-free exchange. In addition, dispositions resulting in a loss (other than from a casualty), as well as operating expenses, cannot be deducted.

Personal residences, however, can be converted into rental properties, but a new basis may have to be established. (See ''Basis'' below.) The new basis is the lesser of (1) fair market value on the date of conversion or (2) your adjusted basis on that date. In order to achieve the status of income-producing property, the property must be offered for rent under ordinary conditions (e.g., it is advertised and rent is set at the fair market rate). Generally, the converted residence must have been actually rented, though, before a loss resulting from a sale can be deducted.

For personal residences converted to income-producing property on or after January 1, 1987 the prevailing cost recovery rules at the time of conversion (27.5 year life under the straight-line method) must be used. Also, once a residence is converted and sold as income producing property, any gain realized will be recognized for tax purposes. Gain on personal residences, on the other hand, can be deferred by purchasing and occupying another residence within the appropriate time period (usually, two years). Gain (up to $125,000) can also be completely excluded for a taxpayer age 55 or older.

Property held for sale by a dealer in the ordinary course of business is inventory. Generally, a real estate developer or a taxpayer who buys residences for the sole purpose of immediately reselling them is typically considered a dealer. Properties held by a dealer as inventory cannot be depreciated, cannot qualify for tax-free exchanges, and generally cannot be donated as a gift to charities at fair market value. Operating expenses and losses from a sale or exchange, however, can be deducted. (Dealers can designate certain properties as held for the production of income if appropriate steps are taken showing this intent— e.g., the designated property is not held out for sale, rented, or kept for a longer period than is customary for inventory property.)

Investors who own rental houses may run the risk of being classified as dealers by the Internal Revenue Service if all properties are put up for sale and proceeds received are used to purchase more houses. The key issue is the intent of the taxpayer in light of all facts and circumstances.

BASIS

Basis is an amount used to determine depreciation, casualty losses, and gain or loss upon disposition. In most instances when property is obtained through outright purchase, the basis is the purchase price. (If property is bought from a "related party," see your tax adviser.) Included in a property's cost of acquisition— and thereby becoming its basis—are the purchase price and the following additional expenses paid by the purchaser:

(1) Broker's commissions (if not already included in the purchase price).
(2) Attorney's fees.
(3) Title charges.
(4) Surveys.
(5) Appraisals.
(6) Cost of renegotiating or acquiring existing leases.
(7) Tax stamps.
(8) Option payments.
(9) Charges resulting from change in zoning.
(10) Accounting services for property acquisition.

If property is inherited or received as a gift, then basis is determined under a different set of rules. Generally, property received from a decedent's estate has a basis equal to its fair market value at the date of death. An alternate valuation date can also be chosen. But in this case, basis is determined using either the date of distribution or the alternate valuation date, whichever is earlier.

Property received as a gift after 1976 will usually have a basis equal to the donor's adjusted basis plus a portion of the gift tax that is attributable to the unrealized appreciation. (However, if fair market value is lower than the donor's basis, then fair market value will be used to compute a loss resulting from an eventual sale by the recipient.)

CAPITALIZED EXPENDITURES VERSUS EXPENSES

Once a property held for the production of income is acquired, there are two separate types of expenditures that must be accounted for: *capitalized expenditures* and *expenses*. Generally, improvements made to a property will increase its basis because they are not immediately deducted. Repairs and maintenance, however, will be routinely deducted as operating expenses.

Improvements usually involve a permanent increase in a property's value or a lengthening of its useful life. Expenditures for the following items ordinarily represent examples of such improvements (capitalized expenditures):

(1) Architect's fees.
(2) Replacing a roof.
(3) Installing new electrical wiring.
(4) Replacing water pipes.
(5) Replacing a permanent heating and/or air-conditioning unit.
(6) Restoring damaged property for a different use.
(7) Restoring damaged property for which insurance proceeds were received and/or tax deductions were taken.
(8) Altering a property for a different use.
(9) Remodeling.
(10) Installing new floors (including carpet).
(11) Installing energy-saving items.
(12) Property assessments by local authorities for improvements (e.g., sidewalks, street paving, street lights).
(13) Landscaping.
(14) Replacing appliances.
(15) Closing costs borne by the purchaser.
(16) Constructing new additions.

Expenses tend to recur and are usually associated with keeping a property in operating condition. When paid by a cash basis taxpayer for property held for the production of income, the following items are generally considered to be expenses:

(1) Painting and wallpapering.
(2) Repairing broken shingles.
(3) Mending defective wiring.
(4) Mending defective pipes.
(5) Stopping plumbing leaks.
(6) Fixing broken windows.
(7) Patching floors.
(8) Replacing broken stairway supports.
(9) Plastering cracks in the walls.
(10) Mowing the lawn and trimming the shrubbery.
(11) Cleaning.
(12) Periodic servicing of the air conditioner (scheduled maintenance).
(13) Replacing broken doors.
(14) Repairing appliances.
(15) Minor resurfacing of driveway.

ADJUSTED BASIS

After a property's cost basis (unadjusted basis) has been established, it is important to consider certain deductible expenses (other than those listed above) which do not require cash outlay but will reduce the property's basis. In addition, certain receipts of cash and other specified events will reduce the basis. Thus, an "adjusted basis" is one that was increased by capitalized expenditures and was decreased by *certain* noncash deductions, cash proceeds, and certain other events. The following items fall into the latter category:

(1) Depreciation deductions.
(2) Casualty loss deductions.
(3) Abandonment deduction.
(4) Insurance proceeds resulting from casualties.
(5) "Sale of an easement" proceeds (beneficial use of land is not affected).

(6)   Qualifying forgiveness of debt.
(7)   Certain allowable tax credits.

DEPRECIATION

In most instances, when a single-family residence is acquired, both a structure and land are involved. As mentioned earlier, land is not depreciable, so the purchase price (or other basis) must be allocated between the building and the land. This can be done using the ratio of their respective fair market values or using their assessed values (as determined by the local tax assessor's office) at the time of purchase. For example, assume you purchased a house on a three-quarter acre lot for $100,000. An independent appraisal of the property showed the land was worth $25,000 and the building was worth $125,000. The depreciable portion of your property's basis would be $83,333 [($125,000/$150,000) x $100,000].

As of January 1, 1987, straight-line depreciation over a 27.5-year life will be used for all residential properties placed in service (31.5 years for nonresidential property). An alternate recovery period, 40 years, is available. An election to depreciate over a 40-year period rather than a 27.5-year period can be made on a property-by-property basis.

A midmonth convention applies, which means that property is deemed to be placed in service (and disposed of) in the middle of the month—regardless of when such property is actually placed in service (or disposed of) during the month. Thus, the first month's (and last month's) separate amount of depreciation will actually be one half that of all other months.

Generally, depreciation of improvements (or additions) begin on the later of (1) the date the improvement was placed in service, or (2) when the property including the improvement was placed in service. Also, the method of depreciation used is the same as is used for the underlying property. However, if a ''substantial improvement'' is made, then it may be depeciated without reference to prior elections on the underlying property (i.e., it may be treated as a separate building). Substantial improvements are those made after the building has been placed in service for at least three years, are made over a 24-month period, and are at least 25 percent of the building's adjusted basis (without regard to depreciation).

PROBLEM V—Depreciation

You already own one rental house and decide to purchase another one for $65,000 in January 1987. You immediately made additional expenditures for the following during the month: attorney's fees at closing ($1,000), replacing the air-conditioning system ($4,000), and cleaning and painting ($500 and $1,000 respectively). In March a new carpet was installed ($2,500) and landscaping was done ($500). How much of these expenditures can be deducted in 1987?

Answer

$4,024

CAPITALIZED EXPENDITURES FOR 1987:	JANUARY	MARCH
Purchase price	$65,000	
Attorney's fees	1,000	
Air conditioner	4,000	
Cleaning	*	
Painting	*	
Carpet		$2,500
Landscaping		500
Total	$70,000	$3,000
Depreciation per month		
(Total × 1/27.5 × 1/12)	$ 212	$ 9
Times total number of months	× 12	× 10
	$2,544	$90
Less one-half month	(106)	(4.5)
	$2,438	$86

*Expensed

Total deduction for 1987:

Depreciation	$2,524 ($2,438 + $86)
Other expenses	1,500
	$4,024

CAPITAL GAINS   The preferred treatment given to long-term capital gains is no longer available for the sale of rental or other investment property. During the 1987 tax year, however, the maximum tax rate for long-term capital gain property is 28 percent. Congress may approve special treatment of the sale of investment property in the future, reinstating preferential treatment.

AT-RISK RULES   In the past, most real estate was purchased with nonrecourse financing, which are loans that are secured solely by the property itself and not the personal assets of the purchaser. Congress has changed the "at-risk" rules to include real estate, which means that an investor is personally liable for debts against real property (also known as recourse financing or debt personally assumed) or must have a qualified loan.

Generally, a real estate investor can now deduct losses from a certain property only to the extent that he or she is at risk in that property. However, if nonrecourse debt is qualified, which means it is covered by a nonrecourse loan that is not convertible debt and is obtained from a qualified lender (qualified lenders are those who are actively engaged in the business of lending money), then losses can be deducted as if the investor were at risk. On the other hand, losses that fall under the at-risk limitation (because the owner is not personally liable or financing is not qualified) will become deductible—subject to the passive loss rules below—when the owner qualifies as being at risk or the debt becomes qualified.

Nonrecourse loans obtained from the seller of the property are an unqualified financing technique, which leaves the purchaser in a position of not being at risk. Conceivably, an investor could later become personally liable for the debt and thereby become at risk. These rules apply to property acquired on or after January 1, 1987.

PASSIVE LOSS LIMITATION   Passive losses are those arising from the conduct of a trade or business in which an individual who would otherwise deduct such losses does not "materially participate." All limited partnership interests and rental activities (other than those where substantial services are rendered, such as operating a hotel) automatically fall into the passive loss category. The renting of single-family homes is a passive activity.

Generally, the rule is that passive losses can only be used as tax deductions against income from passive activities. However, all unused losses are merely "suspended" and can be carried forward indefinitely until they are offset against future passive income or the entire interest is disposed of through a taxable disposition (including an abandonment). Beginning in 1987, there is a four-year phase in of this rule so that a portion of these losses (for passive activities existing before October 22, 1986) can still be deducted through 1990.

Rental real estate activities, though, come under a special rule: Individuals who "actively participate" in rental real estate activities are entitled to deduct up to $25,000 per year of net losses (and/or tax credit equivalents) resulting from that activity. For married taxpayers filing separately and living apart at all times during the tax year, the amount is $12,500 each. These investors must have an adjusted gross income (computed without regard to IRA contributions, net passive losses, or taxable Social Security benefits) of $100,000 or less.

The $25,000 ceiling is phased out at a rate of 50 percent of the amount of adjusted gross income in excess of $100,000. For example, assume a taxpayer has an adjusted gross income of $120,000. The amount of losses that can be deducted is $15,000 [$25,000 − 50% × ($120,000 − $100,000)]. Therefore, a taxpayer whose adjusted gross income is $150,000 or more is not allowed the deduction. Any amount of losses that cannot be deducted are subject to the passive loss rules.

Mortgage interest incurred on rental property can be deducted under the $25,000 loss provision without regard to the investment interest limitation. The investment interest limitation, however, applies to virtually all other investments.

"Active participation" requires that an individual have a 10 percent or more interest in the project and provide significant, bona fide involvement. Such involvement would include approval of tenants, approving repairs and improvements, and setting rental terms. Using a rental agent and a management company is permissible. Generally, if the investor makes important management decisions and exercises independent judgment, he or she is considered to be an active participant. (This book has been directed toward active participants, rather than passive investors.)

The renting of resort condominiums or single-family homes on a daily or weekly basis and providing significant services thereto would not fall under the passive loss limitations if the owner(s) "materially participate" (as opposed to active participation) in the operations of the business on a regular, continuous, and substantial basis. Material participation generally calls for a full-time commitment, and the success of the activity must depend on the exercise of business judgment by the individual. Thus, losses from short-term rentals where services are provided can be deducted against other income.

An investor who has existing passive losses that cannot be deducted currently, however, will need passive income to offset such losses. This investor should consider buying rental properties and avoid being an "active participant" by designating a trustworthy third party to take over *all and absolute* control—including management, maintenance, and selling responsibilities—over the property. By making such a designation, the investor will assume the role of a "passive participant," and be able to receive—tax free—income generated by the rental properties up to the amount of existing or suspended passive losses. In this case, cash flow would be the primary objective, so that increased amounts of equity would be needed to fund the acquisitions.

INSTALLMENT SALES Collecting payments from the sale of real property in more than one tax year constitutes an installment sale, if no election was made to treat the sale differently. Generally, as each payment is received, one portion will be taxable (resulting from a gain on sale of the property), another portion will be taxable as interest, and the remaining portion is considered to be a tax-free return of capital. This arrangement allows the seller to report and pay taxes on the gain over a period of years rather than paying all taxes due in the year of sale. A large percentage of real estate sales have been made using the installment method through which the seller receives a cash down payment in the year of sale and the balance with interest over a period of years. If the equitable provisions of the installment sale rules were not available, many sellers would find themselves with a cash-flow problem, particularly when large profits are involved.

An important element in installment obligations is the interest received by the seller. Generally, if interest is below the applicable federal rate or 9 percent at the time of the loan, then the IRS may impute interest.

Another major aspect of using installment sales is that closing costs are reduced to a minimum: Usually held to any attorney's fees due (which run anywhere from $200 up depending on the services rendered) and the cost of a survey. In addition, no points are involved. If an existing loan is to be assumed, however, the lender may require an assumption fee as stated in the lending agreement.

The formula for computing the taxable portion of a receipt from an installment sale is as follows:

$$\text{Gross profit/Contract price} \times \text{Payment received}$$

Gross profit is the selling price less selling expenses and less adjusted basis. The contract price is the selling price less any qualifying indebtedness that does not exceed the basis of the property sold. Such indebtedness includes all mortgage debt assumed or taken "subject to" (i.e., not at risk) by the purchaser.

For example, assume you are selling a property for $100,000, and you are financing the sale. Your adjusted basis in the property is $67,000 and a $40,000 loan is to be assumed by the purchaser. Selling expenses amounted to $3,000. During the year of sale, you receive a $5,000 down payment and installment payments totaling $2,000 (of which $1,800 is interest). The amount of taxable gain to report is $2,600 and the remaining $2,600 is a tax-free return of capital computed as follows:

Selling price	$100,000
Less: Selling expenses	(3,000)
Adjusted basis	(67,000)
Gross profit	$30,000
Selling price	$100,000
Less: Debt assumed	(40,000)
Contract price	$60,000

Taxable portion
of down payment = ($30,000/$60,000) × $5,000 = $2,500

Taxable portion
of other payments = ($30,000/$60,000) × $200 = 100

Tax-Free Return of Capital $2,600

Therefore, of the $7,000 received during the year of sale, $1,800 is interest, $2,600 is taxable gain from sale, and the remaining $2,600, as stated, is a tax-free return of capital.

There is an important caveat for users of installment sales: If the selling price of real property held for production of income exceeds $150,000, then a "deemed payment" resulting from the installment sale may be involved. The deemed payment or "allocable installment indebtedness" on the note is based on the seller's outstanding debt. Because of this burdensome effect, installment reporting of income may not be a practical alternative for property valued over $150,000 if the seller has a significant amount of debt.

PROBLEM VI – INSTALLMENT SALE

You sold a single-family residence for $125,000, which had an existing mortgage balance of $90,000. You purchased it two years ago for $105,000 and deducted depreciation of $7,318. Selling expenses amounted to $3,000. During the year of sale you received a $6,000 down payment and $5,000 in installments (of which $4,600 was interest). How much of the $11,000 received during the year of sale is taxable?

Answer

$9,047 ($4,600 + $4,447)

(1) Interest = $4,600

(2) Gross profit = $24,318
= [$125,000 − ($105,000 − $7,318) − $3,000]

(3) Contract price = $35,000
= ($125,000 − $90,000)

(4) Taxable portion
of installments
& down payment = $4,447
= [$24,318/$35,000 × $6,400]

TAX-FREE EXCHANGE

Rental properties can be traded without tax consequences in accordance with the rules covering a like-kind exchange. Like-kind properties include all real property held for investment or the production of income (including raw land), and real property must be traded for real property. Your personal residence will not qualify for this type of exchange. Examples include a single-family residence held for the production of income traded for a duplex held for the same purpose, an apartment building for building lots, and a farm for a farm. Personalty, however, cannot be traded for realty to avoid taxation under this provision.

Generally, there is no tax liability from a like-kind exchange unless boot (unlike property, such as cash) is *received*. Even then, the amount of gain "recognized" can only equal the amount of gain "realized" from the exchange. Gain realized is the difference between the exchanged property's fair market value and its adjusted basis. Gain recognized is the lesser of (1) boot received or (2) gain realized. If boot is given—and none is received—then no gain is recognized (hence, no tax is due).

Having a mortgage assumed or taken subject to on property you are exchanging is the equivalent of receiving boot. This mortgage, however, can be offset by any mortgages assumed or taken subject to on the new property. Therefore, exchanging a highly leveraged property for another property, which has very little or no debt, may not be worthwhile.

ALTERNATIVE MINIMUM TAX

Generally, the alternative minimum tax (AMT) will not affect most individuals because of the elimination of the preferential treatment of long-term capital gains and the availability of an exclusive exemption. However, those who have substantial holdings in depreciable assets, passive-activity losses, and/or a rather large amount of taxable income (e.g., in excess of $150,000) may be adversely affected because of the compression of individual income tax rates (28 percent regular tax versus 21 percent AMT).

The alternative minimum tax is imposed to ''assure'' that certain individuals, namely those who were able to avoid income taxes through the use of preferential treatment of investment items, such as accelerated depreciation on rental properties, pay some tax. It has the effect of eliminating many crucial tax-reducing particulars,and thereby taxing individuals at a flat 21 percent rate for amounts that could not be excluded under the new provisions.

Other elements targeted by the AMT include installment sales (taxpayers cannot defer taxable gains into the future), appreciated donations to charity, and a certain type of tax-exempt interest. Be sure to consult your tax adviser on this matter before you invest. You may have to keep track of tax preference items and AMT adjustments even though no current AMT tax liability exists: future AMT computations may require it.

Chapter
Six

FINANCING, MANAGEMENT, AND SELLING

FINANCING

A common policy for many financial institutions is to lend up to 80 percent of the appraised value (loan-to-value or L/V ratio) of an investment property. However, not all lenders adhere to this rule, and on some occasions, favorable financing, generally up to 90 percent L/V, can be obtained. When a seller participates with a second (or sometimes first) mortgage, an even higher L/V ratio is possible.

SOURCES OF FUNDING

THE FEDERAL HOUSING ADMINISTRATION (FHA)   The Federal Housing Administration originated the practice of making long-term loans for residential real estate. However, the FHA does not actually lend money, it insures loans. FHA loans are handled through commercial banks, savings and loans, mortgage bankers, and other qualified lenders. Even though many conventional financing techniques do not strictly follow the Federal Housing Administration's lending guidelines, most bear some resemblance to the FHA's basic lending practices.

A service of the FHA for investors is the authority to insure loans for residential rental properties. Although the amounts are subject to change and may vary from location to location, the FHA will insure up to $90,000 for a 30-year loan at the prevailing market rate. Generally, the maximum L/V for investors not occupying the residence is 85 percent of the cost of acquisition (purchase price plus closing costs) or the FHA appraised value, whichever is less.

One characteristic of an FHA loan is the ability of the borrower to finance the mortgage insurance premium (MIP). The borrower has the option of either paying all or part of the premium at closing and adding any balance to the loan, having someone else pay it in full, or adding it to the amount borrowed (without regard to the L/V ratio or maximum loan amount). The amount of an FHA mortgage insurance premium on a 30-year mortgage is 3.8 percent of the loan. Private mortgage insurance (PMI), on the other hand, involves fewer conditions, but normally requires the premium to be paid in cash by either the buyer or seller at closing. Generally, higher loans can be made by lenders when mortgage insurance is obtained. As a general rule, L/V ratios of 80 percent or less do not require mortgage insurance.

FHA loans do not contain a "due on sale" clause. Such a clause has the effect of accelerating payment of any unpaid principal as of the next sale. FHA loans also do not contain a prepayment penalty. Obtaining a second loan to provide the required cash down payment for a new FHA mortgage is prohibited, but obtaining a second loan to fund a down payment in order to assume an existing FHA loan is acceptable. An "open end" provision can be arranged, which allows the borrower to receive advances for improvements or repairs.

Potential buyers must generally meet three qualifications: they must have a satisfactory credit record, possess the required amount of cash for down payment and closing costs, and have the ability to meet their financial obligation. Rental properties are treated as a business, and only the net amount of income, not including depreciation and income taxes, will increase the "net effective income" figure.

The FHA has set strict standards in appraising properties. The appraisal factors include square footage, location, and condition. If any repairs, reconditioning, or alterations are needed, they must be completed before closing. Even minimum FHA standards for carpeting have been set.

FHA provisions, rates, standards, guidelines, etc., are continually changing. Therefore, we suggest that a current survey be made of these services by contacting the local FHA office or your local lender. This information is important when selling real estate as well as when buying.

Mortgage Bankers   The **mortgage banker** (or mortgage company) locates and qualifies borrowers, completes the paperwork for applications, and makes loans. Typically, mortgage bankers keep and service only a very small portion of loans, selling a much greater number in the secondary markets (such as the Federal National Mortgage Association—FNMA—or "Fannie Mae") where government agencies, lending institutions, and investors buy and sell huge blocks of existing mortgages. Because of mortgage insurance and standardized mortgage arrangements, such a market exists, which in turn, allows lenders to sell their mortgages.

Only the largest companies can provide a full range of lending services. Some of the smaller ones have become highly specialized in only a few of these services such as commercial lending, residential properties for owner/occupants, rural property, etc. However, most will be thoroughly familiar with federal regulations relating to FHA and VA (Veterans Administration) loans, the overall availability of mortgage money, the prime and secondary mortgage markets, guidelines for qualifying, and the local real estate market.

Mortgage brokers are middlemen: They bring qualified borrowers and lenders together. Mortgage brokers do not lend money, but they do provide services to the lender and borrower by qualifying the borrower and performing all the administrative activities for loan applications. They do not service the mortgage. For this, the borrower pays a fee ranging from 1 percent to 3 percent of the loan.

ACTUAL FINANCING

Commercial Banks—As the federal and state banking laws continue to change, **commerical banks** appear to be increasingly interested in residential investing. Because most of their funds come from cash deposits, though, they are required by law to keep sufficient amounts in reserves and high-quality investments that can be readily liquidated so that cash-deposit accounts can be served. Due to this situation, commercial banks are usually more interested in relatively short-term residential lending, such as construction loans, home improvement loans, and home equity loans.

As is true with most financial institutions, commercial banks do not have a uniform set of policies regarding real estate investments. Some banks, usually in rural and isolated locations, can and do provide home mortgage money. Many of the larger banks provide mortgages for long-term investments as a service to preferred customers, or they have a subsidiary mortgage company originate such loans.

Insurance Companies—In recent years, **life insurance companies** have actively sought to make loans in real estate. The procedures for acquiring a loan vary widely between companies, but most have stopped providing loans for residences.

Loans from insurance companies are usually made through a loan correspondent (i.e., a commerical lending institution) which, generally, has paid a fee for making and servicing loans for real estate investments. Even though most companies specialize only in large-scale projects and prefer to loan in blocks of millions of dollars, some of the local companies are interested in community development projects and will provide funds in lesser amounts for rental properties. An investor who is interested in getting loans from a life insurance company may receive information from a local lender, a life insurance company, or the state department of insurance.

S&Ls—**Savings and loan associations** are also known by other names such as saving associations, homestead associations, and cooperative banks and can be either state or federally chartered. S&Ls are similar to commercial banks in that they are allowed to provide passbook savings accounts, set up interest-bearing checking accounts, and issue certificates of deposit. Their focus, however, is residential properties for owner/occupants, but construction, investor, and commercial real estate loans can be made through most savings and loans.

Mutual Savings Banks—In many states, **mutual savings banks** compete with other institutions in the real estate investment market. Usually state chartered, they operate under guidelines for federal agencies and provide much the same services for real estate operations as the other primary mortgage institutions. As the name "mutual" implies, the depositors own the bank and share in its successes or failures. These banks are mostly located in the Northeast and are a prime source of real estate investment funds.

Other Sources—Other sources of real estate investment money include **pension funds**, **trust funds** (including real estate investment trusts), **finance companies**, and **credit unions**. Each source has its own restrictions and practices for making loans.

Private sources of funding play a significant role in real estate. Private funding can come from family members, friends, interested investors, and perhaps more importantly, the seller. As mentioned in Chapter 5, when a property is completely financed through private means, there are no points and closing costs are minimal. Leads for private sources may come from acquaintances, friends, business associates, newspaper ads, etc.

An example of this type of funding occurred when a seasoned real estate investor put down $20,000, secured a loan for the balance of the purchase price, and bought a 25-year-old house needing repairs. It had once been an expensive dwelling located in a high-priced neighborhood. A home improvement contractor agreed to put this house in like-new condition—including repairing the lawn, walkways, and driveway—for $42,000, money the investor did not have. Avoiding a second mortgage, she formed a joint venture with an acquaintance, who agreed to pay the $42,000 for 20 percent of the net profit after the house was sold. They estimated that it should sell for somewhere over $235,000.

Twelve months later, the house sold for a net selling price of $220,000. The joint venture realized $70,000 with the co-venturer receiving $14,000, a 33.33 percent gain; the originating investor received $56,000 for a 280 percent gain on her $20,000 investment. The investor had and used the expertise to recognize the opportunity, the initiative to exploit it, and the knowledge of financing it without risking too much of her own money.

TYPES OF LOANS

After an investor decides that it is advantageous to obtain a loan and secure it with a mortgage, two important decisions must be made: (1) the source of funding, and (2) what kind of loan. At least one mortgage banker and/or one mortgage broker should be called for the purpose of providing additional options and to check current lending practices. Perhaps the financing packages of a commercial bank or even a local real estate investment trust should be investigated. Most people employed in such firms are quite willing to provide useful information and answer many questions over the phone. Another ready reference is a newspaper that carries the local home mortgage rates/points available from local sources. The types of loans vary with the imagination of their originators. Some of the different kinds of loans include the standard mortgage, balloon mortgage, buy-down mortgage, and wraparound mortgage.

Standard Mortgage—The **standard amortized mortgage** is the most common type of financing for residential property. To amortize a mortgage is to eliminate it by making scheduled payments that slowly decrease the principal over the initial period of the loan. The length (term) of the mortgage is any duration agreed on by the mortgagor and the mortgagee. The scheduled payments amortizing the mortgage can be at a fixed rate of interest over the entire term or can change from time to time, as in an adjustable rate mortgage. It is the amount, term, and annual percentage rate (APR) that determine the level of the payment.

Balloon Mortgage—Generally, a **balloon mortgage** (or ''partially amortized loan'') is virtually any lending arrangement which calls for a rather large final payment. This payment is the loan's principal balance which remains because the loan was not fully amortized. When interest rates are high, balloon mortgages are sometimes offered by lenders as a way to make high-interest-rate loans more affordable. Balloon mortgages can be used any time, however, with a seller who agrees to take back a second mortgage (junior mortgage).

As an example of a balloon mortgage: an investor purchases a house for, say, $110,000, and plans to sell it within three years. The terms worked out with the seller are as follows: $10,000 down, five-year balloon mortgage with a monthly payment of $734 ($100,000 principal, 8 percent rate, 30-year amortization). At the end of five years, the entire principal balance ($95,280) will be due. This fits nicely into the investor's plans because he intends to either sell the property within three years or simply refinance it at the end of five years. One of the advantages of a balloon note is that below-market financing (short-term rates) can sometimes be obtained.

Another example of a balloon mortgage is an **interest-only loan**. Take the previous example and change the note to an interest-only instrument, and the monthly payment would be lowered to only $667 (all of it could be currently deductible interest); a balloon payment of $100,000 would be due in five years.

ARM—The **adjustable rate mortgage (ARM)** is an alternative to the standard fixed-payment loan. It is generally used for the purchase of a home. The payments are fixed for a short duration, anywhere from six months to five years, and then increase or decrease in relation to changes in a selected money market index, like U.S. Treasury bills. The actual use of an ARM varies widely among lenders and can cause hardships for the uninformed borrower. ARM's are still quite popular, especially among young families who are in a position to expect their incomes to grow.

Buy-Down Mortgage—The **buy-down mortgage**, sometimes referred to as buy-down financing, buy-down interest, or simply a buy-down, is a method for lowering the initial monthly payments on a long-term mortgage. This is done by making an advanced, lump-sum payment that reflects the present value of the difference between two interest rates over a specified period, usually one to three years. This payment is customarily made by the seller in order to close the deal. When selling a house, a buy-down mortgage can be used to help the purchasers qualify for the loan or can entice would-be purchasers to go ahead and buy.

Wraparound Mortgage—A **wraparound mortgage** is generally considered a seller's tool, but it also has some advantages for the buyer. It is a subordinate, all-inclusive mortgage that encompasses both the first mortgage, which remains undisturbed, and the owner's equity. To be profitable to the seller, the wraparound mortgage should have a higher interest rate than the first mortgage. These mortgages are desirable when a seller is anxious, a buyer cannot otherwise qualify for a loan, a buyer has little or no down payment, the seller has a firm price but the terms are flexible, or when there is little or no time to qualify for a new mortgage. Wraparounds may not be used, however, when there is a "due on sale" clause written in any of the notes, trust deeds, or security deeds associated with the property to be sold. Wraparounds fall under the installment sale provisions of the Internal Revenue Code.

An example of a wraparound would involve a seller who owns property having a 7 percent, $40,000 first mortgage which he sells for $100,000, with a 10 percent cash down payment and a 30-year note covering the balance. The rate of interest stated in the second note is the prevailing market rate of interest at that time, which is 12 percent. Obviously the seller would not wish to pay off his $40,000 loan (for which he remains personally liable) because of its attractive interest rate. The buyer, on the other hand, is pleased because he does not want to be personally liable for repayment of the note: In the event of default, the seller agrees to look only at the subject property. Thus, the seller receives $10,000 and takes a $90,000 second mortgage bearing interest at a rate greater than that of the first mortgage. The $90,000 mortgage ''wraps around'' the first mortgage ($40,000) as well as a portion of the seller's equity ($50,000).

A seller should check with his or her tax adviser concerning possible changes in the law, court decisions, or IRS rulings. In addition, sellers should consult with their real estate attorneys to make sure that a wraparound can be used and to draw up the necessary documents. Items to be stated in the arrangement may include a provision for the seller to have the right to approve all leases, limit or forbid the use of another wraparound (e.g., include a ''due on sale'' clause), and spell out precise default procedures and how the amount in default is to be determined.

Buyers should be aware that a nonrecourse loan from a seller will prevent the latter from being ''at risk'' (see Chapter 5). In addition, the buyer should take steps to ensure that the seller will make timely payments on the first mortgage (e.g., buyer makes payments to an escrow account held by a trust or neutral third party and the release of such funds are contingent upon the seller's payment on the first mortgage).

MANAGEMENT

Property management requires patience. Complete management means phone calls at 12:45 A.M. from a tenant who has a leaky faucet, frequent visits to the property, locating tenants who moved out without paying rent, and a host of good reasons why a rent payment is delayed. The first inspection of a property is an initial step in property management. Records are to be kept in detail for each house with all the necessary information needed for future decisions. The cash-flow analysis (Chapters 3 and 4) begins this process.

Frequently, an investor will want to reconsider his overall objective and increase the size of the portfolio beyond its original projection, or the original size selected may be beyond the capabilities of the investor. In either case, professional management or the services of a real estate consultant must be considered in the early going.

After your first property is acquired, you must immediately decide what role you want to take in managing the property. Then, prepare to select a real estate management company that fits into your plans. Most companies are specialized in only one or two types of properties. Some are small operations within an organization holding properties of its own. The largest companies have highly qualified personnel in all types of property management (accounting, maintenance, marketing, etc.). Many management companies are part of a real estate agency and can provide the services of a real estate broker. Some of the different services offered include total property management, negotiating leases, accounting services, collecting rents, marketing the property, maintenance and repairs (painting, recarpeting, etc.), showing the property, and otherwise managing the day-to-day affairs. Shop around and select the one that not only meets your criteria, but which you can comfortably work with as well.

RISK MANAGEMENT The purpose of risk management is to maintain existing assets by keeping their exposure to risks at a minimum. Additionally, a periodic review of expenses should be done to see if there is a less expensive, but just as effective, way to operate the venture.

Common risks that can affect your investment include physical hazards, liability suits, holding an invalid title, stable or declining property value, inability to rent at a fair rate, and spending too much money.

Little managerial effort is required to avoid certain risks, such as physical hazards, liability suits, and holding an invalid title. Each of these can be taken care of with a separate insurance policy (hazard and liability insurance are frequently combined in one policy). Be sure to review the coinsurance provisions of your hazard insurance policy because you must maintain a certain amount of insurance in terms of the value of your property. When selling your property, have an exculpatory clause written in the appropriate document(s) to help avoid liability in the event of future lawsuits against the property owner(s).

Avoiding a failure of your property to increase in value, not being able to rent, and preventing spendthrift tendencies require much more managerial skill and talent.

Keep each unit insured against loss or damages that cannot be transferred to the tenant. Require each tenant to maintain insurance coverage for all loss and damage claims for which the occupant can be legally held liable; the premiums for tenant insurance may be included in the lease contract and collected as part of the monthly rent. (Do not commingle premiums collected with rental payments but hold them in escrow.) If possible, lease to long-term tenants (one year or longer) and make suitable accommodations for those who are forced to vacate for circumstances beyond their control. Such leases will help eliminate the risk of short-term occupancy with long-term vacancies as well as reduce undue wear and tear on the property.

The lease should: be written in simple, easy-to-read English; contain an escalation clause stating that rent may increase with rises in inflation, additional taxation, and/or escalating insurance premiums; prohibit any home improvements by tenants unless approved by the landlord; require a deposit of at least one month's payment to be held in escrow (along with any insurance premiums) which is to be returned to the tenant when he or she vacates the property, provided the property is left clean and in the same condition as it was when the tenant moved in—with the exception of normal wear and tear.

Purchase property below the estimated market price of a similar property and establish full equity as rapidly as practical where rental income is the objective; keep equity to a minimum where resale is the objective. Continue to seek better and improved financing techniques for purchases, refinancing, and sales. Diversify your purchases by acquiring homes in different neighborhoods and that differ in value. Continually update and expand your records on each house in your portfolio.

The mechanics of setting up the records and keeping them updated will require increasing amounts of time as the project grows. From the beginning, you need a system for keeping such records in a manner that allows for expansion with little or no additional upkeep time for the investor: Use a personal computer or employ a specialist!

There are two reasons for keeping records: one is to satisfy the requirements of the Internal Revenue Service to show how your taxes were computed, and the other is to provide information for decision making at a later date. Records should include:

1. All the required financial summaries on each unit, including depreciation, improvements, expenses allocated to, etc.
2. A summary of and a detailed report on each inspection to the property, including a statement about the tenants.
3. A record of each complaint about the property from tenants, and a statement of the manager's reaction.
4. An estimate of the market value of each unit made at least once every three years.
5. A detailed statement of action taken by management to enhance the property, increase its income, and/or reduce expenses.

SELLING

If you plan to sell the property yourself, you might consider, at least initially, paying a seasoned real estate agent (or broker) a consulting fee for helping to sell and close the property. Special forms and certain procedures are necessary and timing is always of the essence. Having such a professional guide you through all the steps will prove to be quite helpful, if not absolutely necessary.

Preparations for selling a rental property actually start when the house is made ready for the first renter and continue until the house is finally sold. The ideal rental house for selling is one that has been in your portfolio for seven to eight years, has had all major repairs done within the last three to five years, is to be vacant at the end of the current lease, and is marketable (perhaps as commercial property). If major repairs and/or maintenance have been delayed until the unit is vacant, coordinate these efforts with other jobs to insure there are no undue delays.

The objective is to make the home attractive and inviting in terms of similar properties in the area without having to spend too much. Little things will help, like keeping the utilities connected, having light bulbs in every light socket and all the switches in working order. The entrance should be bright and clean, as should all walls, windows, floors, and ceilings. Sometimes it will pay to have new appliances in the kitchen, new fixtures in the bathrooms, and new carpets on some of the floors. The exterior should be clean with the lawn neatly trimmed. In other words, this house should be a standout in the neighborhood.

You are now an investor selling your own property, which is one of the legal rights of complete ownership. In the colorful parlance of real estate professionals, your unit has become a "fiz bo" (FSBO or "For Sale By Owner"). This can work to your advantage because a really nice property will get the attention of real estate agents, who will constantly call you about it. Never turn away a real estate agent when you are trying to sell real estate. Instead, tell them that you prefer to sell the property yourself. However, should they have a prospect in mind or would like to show the property (by appointment), then you would be interested in paying a commission *provided they can close the deal*.

One of the biggest reasons "fiz bos" do not sell very many houses is that they have over-priced the property. Be sure to know your real estate market well enough so that the house can be priced right.

In addition, have a *professionally painted* sign on the property. The sign should be placed in the front yard, and should say that the property will be shown by appointment only. It should also list your phone number to call for further information. If open houses are popular in this community, hold this unit open every convenient weekend and holiday until it is sold.

Advertise in the local newspapers and on bulletin boards at laundromats and neighborhood grocery stores. Your guide in advertising is to avoid overspending. Don't advertise in local newspapers more than two or three successive times. (Then delay for a few days, start over, and improve the ad.) In each ad be sure to include the number of bedrooms, bathrooms, whether or not the unit has a living room, dining room, family room, fireplace, and garage; the price; and make a remark about the desirability of the house, the neighborhood, and whether special financing is available; then list your telephone number. Do not include the address, square footage, and all the particulars. You only want interested parties to visit the house, but you also want to leave out some good aspects in order to make it appear even better than what was stated in the ad.

The buyer of a single-family house is seldom certain about the exact house that he or she really wants. Also, very few are knowledgeable about the real estate market or available financing arrangements. The basic principle in selling real estate is to make the prospective buyer feel comfortable and perhaps a little excited about the prospects of owning the property.

The technique for selling will differ with individuals, but the basic principle is the same for everyone. For many people a little exaggeration about the good features of the home, a few well-placed compliments to the prospective buyer, and some relatively subtle remarks about how a house like this suggests that the owner is moving up in the world will go a long way toward selling the house.

Be sure, however, not to oversell. Too many sellers tend to go too far and come on too strong. They want to escort prospective buyers all around their house, showing all the wonderful features. Don't do it, because this will make your prospect feel uncomfortable. Include all unique or appealing features in your specially prepared fact sheet.

Almost every home buyer is primarily interested in the amount required for a down payment and the cost of monthly payments. The person buying for the second or third time will often ask specifics about mortgages and interest rates on the house, closing costs, mortgage insurance premiums, etc.— items that are directly related to the initial and amortized expenses. When a potential buyer asks about the price, the investor should be ready to talk finances. This person may be interested in buying, or it may be just idle conversation; in either case, take it seriously. Be prepared to break the price down to terms, such as the monthly payment (principal and interest) along with property taxes and insurance and the approximate amount necessary to close (down payment, mortgage insurance, closing costs, points, transfer taxes, etc.).

When you invite a prospect into the house, give him or her a fact sheet. Since you have been inspecting and buying houses, you already have a format in the fact sheets you have received.

In addition, prepare an information sheet for your purposes. It should contain information on loans and interest rates available, minimum down payments required, and an estimate on monthly payments for taxes and insurance that is slightly higher than the actual costs. Always have your comprehensive, amortized mortgage payment tables, blank forms for determining estimated payments, forms for qualifying the buyer, sales contract (or purchase agreement) forms, and a few sheets of clean paper on which to figure; a real estate calculator is certainly a worthwhile device to keep on hand.

Remember, the prospective buyer must be made to feel at ease in your presence. A good way to do this is to let him or her do the talking. Learn as much as you can about the family, including the occupation of both, if the buyer is married. Continue to ask questions like, ''What do you think about the size of the master bedroom?'' or ''Do you think your wife will like this kitchen?'' or ''Is there plenty of cabinet space?'' When the visit is drawing to an end and no mention has been made about the price, ask one more question about whether or not the prospect has any interest in buying this house.

When the question of price is raised, your reply should suggest continued inquiry from the potential buyer. You may say something like, ''Well, it will depend on the financial arrangements you want to make. The asking price is $82,500.'' (If this information is on the fact sheet, you may withhold the sheet until something about the price is mentioned.) The buyer should reply to your suggestion about financial arrangements if he or she is interested. If the reply is something like, ''We prefer a little larger (better, newer, smaller) house,'' this may indicate a financial problem. Such a reply may indicate that you can help them buy this house, if they desire, as you are planning to finance it yourself.

As soon as you can, have the interested buyer seated at your table. (You will need a small table and at least three chairs that are left in the house until the property is sold.) The first thing to do is determine the qualifications of the buyer for obtaining a mortgage—even though you may plan on financing this sale. This task is accomplished by filling out a borrower's qualification form which you have obtained from a mortgage institution or real estate agent. Most mortgage bankers would be happy to qualify your prospects for you over the telephone (hoping to make the loan themselves).

As you glance over the completed qualification sheet, note whether or not this buyer appears to qualify for a mortgage under FHA guidelines. If it appears that the buyer may not qualify, continue with your financing information (e.g., down payment and monthly payments for FHA financing). Also include a few statements about the down payment and monthly costs for a conventional loan. (You can gather this information from a few mortgage companies.) If the buyer indicates a desire to make an offer, fill in the sales contract giving yourself 48 hours to make a decision. (You can obtain a contract from your real estate agent or attorney.) Never make a snap judgment about accepting or rejecting an offer until you have made an investigation of the buyer's financial status.

If a purchaser appears to be qualified, start filling in the sales contract. At the same time, inform this buyer that you are reducing the asking price. Tell him or her that since you are making a direct sale without having to pay a real estate agent's commission, you are passing on that savings to the buyer.

Some purchasers are reluctant to use any form you may have and prefer to consult their own attorney instead. No problem, but you may want your attorney to review the details of the contract before accepting the offer.

Ask about the earnest money (commitment) to be deposited and held in escrow when you reach the space for this item on the sales contract. It is a good policy to always explain exactly what this payment constitutes and that it is necessary to make a commitment to buy the property. As a general rule, the more earnest money that can be collected, the better off you are in getting the sale closed. If the buyer is using his or her own attorney, have earnest money collected as a requirement either before acceptance or as a counter proposal.

Where the buyer makes an offer to purchase at a price less than the one you gave, fill in the purchase price and continue with the form. Then allow yourself at least 48 hours to make a decision. Do not refuse the offer and return the contract. Instead, make a counter offer by initialling any changes made to the document. Follow the same procedure when any item is unacceptable. When the buyer accepts the asking price and agrees with the terms in the contract, take the buyer to your office and have the signatures, his or hers (as they would have it in the deed) and yours (as signed in the deed), either witnessed or notarized as required by state law; you have now completed the sale and have only the closing left to finish the deal.

Deposit the earnest money in an escrow account, and take the properly signed sales contract to your attorney. After completing all the requirements for transfer of title, your attorney will notify you about a suitable closing date. When the date is determined, notify the buyer of the time, date, and place of the closing as well as the manner of payment and amounts he or she will need to bring for the transfer of the deed. This notification should be in writing.

Chapter
Seven

COMPREHENSIVE PROBLEM: COMPARATIVE ANALYSIS

THE PURCHASE

After a reasonable search, you have found a prospective property that meets your nonfinancial criteria, including the appropriate amenities, good neighborhood, proximity to shopping areas, etc. Prior to the search, however, you determined that your investment plan calls for value appreciation and some cash flow. Assuming you have a moderate amount of risk tolerance, quite a bit of available cash, and a small amount of knowledge of real estate projects, you feel reasonably ready to invest. You plan to be an "active participant," at least enough to avoid the passive loss limitation for federal income tax purposes.

One major concern, however, is whether to invest a certain lump sum amount in *one* rental property or invest only 10 percent of the purchase price and leave the balance in a relatively safe investment earning the prevailing market rate of interest. You want to know whether the cash flow from rentals will be more favorable than leaving the balance in its current investment position. If so, is it significant enough to warrant purchasing the property without financing it?

For purposes of the exercise, the amount you are considering is $135,000, and the market rate of interest your funds are presently earning is 7 percent before income taxes (5.04 percent after taxes).

119

Cash flow is a factor only if the real estate project can considerably outperform the existing 5.04 percent rate of return, taking on more risk will certainly be a major factor in making the decision. Should a comparative analysis show that a 100 percent equity purchase is better than all other choices, say by at least 4 percent annual return, then you would purchase the property without leveraging it.

The house you are ready to buy can be purchased for $135,000, with 10 percent down and a 90 percent loan at 8.7 percent over 30 years (PI is $952). The estimated rate of value increase per annum is 6 percent. Fair monthly rental is $1,100, and it is estimated to increase at a rate of 3 percent per year. Vacancies and credit losses are reasonably estimated at 10 percent, and annual operating expenses are $2,000 (increasing at a rate of 10 percent per year). Your marginal tax bracket is 28 percent, and your required rate of return for such an investment is 26 percent when leveraged (90 percent loan) and 12 percent if the property is purchased outright.

The depreciation method is straight line over a 27.5 year life, and 92 percent of the purchase price is allocated to the structure. Selling expenses are expected to be 3 percent of the eventual selling price. You plan to hold the house for exactly four years.

Your alternatives are as follows:

(A) Keep your present investment.
(B) Purchase the property without borrowing any funds.
(C) Purchase the property with a 90 percent loan.

First, may we suggest that you prepare a cash-flow (feasibility) analysis using the variables above. An analysis should be made for the latter two alternatives (B and C) and should answer the question "will the required rate of return be equal to or greater than the project's internal rate of return?"

Second, you should make a comparative analysis showing the future value of cash flow from all three alternatives. The reinvestment rate for the last two alternatives, however, should be 5.04 percent, because this is the rate you are presently earning on your money.

Comparative Analysis

A) PRESENT INVESTMENT
FUTURE VALUE OF $135,000 @ 5.04% AFTERTAX RATE OF RETURN (4 YEARS)
      TOTAL FUTURE VALUE OF INVESTMENT
         $= \$135{,}000 \times (1.0504)^4$
         $= \underline{\$164{,}344}$

B) 100% EQUITY
FUTURE VALUE OF OUTRIGHT PURCHASE
(CASH FLOWS @ 5.04% + SALE PROCEEDS)

YEAR	CASH FLOW	FV FACTOR	FV
1	$8,325	1.0504^3	$9,648
2	$8,491	1.0504^2	$9,368
3	$8,597	1.0504	$9,030
4	$8,642	1	$8,642
4	$151,878	1	$151,878

TOTAL FV OF INVESTMENT $188,566

C) 10% EQUITY & 90% LOAN
FUTURE VALUE OF SALES PROCEEDS (W/90% LEVERAGE) AND
$121,500 @ 5.04% (4 YEARS)

FV OF CASH FLOWS (SAME FACTORS AS ABOVE):

1	($113)	1.158949	($131)
2	$0	1.103340	$0
3	$41	1.050400	$43
4	$40	1.000000	$40
4	$34,416	1.000000	$34,416

TOTAL FV OF REINVESTMENT $34,368
TOTAL FV OF BALANCE @ 5.04%* $147,909

TOTAL FV OF INVESTMENT $182,277

*TOTAL FV OF BALANCE @ 5.04%:

$= \$121{,}500 \times (1.0504)^4$
$= \$147{,}909$

After considering the cash-flow analysis, choice *C* seems to be the better alternative of the two real estate options because its 26 percent required rate of return is feasible. Alternative *B*'s 12 percent required rate, on the other hand, was not attainable under the conditions specified. Note the Net Present Value in alternative *B* was −$12,665, which means you would be paying too much by that amount.

In the comparative analysis, alternative *B* will return a slightly higher amount after four years. Using the future value figures generated in the comparison, the aftertax rate of return for all three alternatives is as follows:

(*A*) 5.04%
(*B*) 8.72%
(*C*) 7.80%

One relevant concern you had was whether putting the entire $135,000 into the project would create more risk of loss: most definitely! Any time real estate is purchased without financing, the risk of loss is greater than when purchasing with a *nonrecourse* loan and a down payment. Why? Because with a nonrecourse note, the lender cannot invade your personal assets if the note is not paid off—you are not personally liable. Only the property (i.e., your down payment) will be taken by the lender if foreclosure became necessary. Thus, by keeping 90 percent of your assets in a relatively safe investment and using only 10 percent in a riskier real estate deal, you could still come within 1 percentage point of the rate of return generated by an outright purchase. Your answer should now be quite clear: Buy the property with a 90 percent loan, take on very little risk, and enjoy a handsome return on the entire $135,000.

What would be the outcome if you were to purchase 10 properties similar to the one just analyzed for your $135,000? Would you be diversified? Could you afford the mortgage payment for a couple of months because of vacancies in say two houses? Would you experience a 26% rate of return if you variables turn out to be accurate? Would pyramiding better suit your investment style?

Appendix
A

BIBLIOGRAPHY

"Apartment Market Outlook," *National Real Estate Investor* (annual).

Allen, Robert G. *Nothing Down*, rev. ed. New York: Simon and Schuster, 1984.

Faggen, Ivan, et. al. *Federal Taxes Affecting Real Estate*. 5th ed. New York: Mathew Bender, 1986.

Friedman, Edith J. *Real Estate Encyclopedia*, rev. ed. Englewood Cliffs, NJ: Prentice-Hall, 1978.

Gaines, George, Jr., & David S. Coleman. *Florida Real Estate Principles, Practices & Law Instructor's Manual*, 9th ed. Chicago: Real Estate Education Company, 1985.

Hanrahan, Michael J. "Merits of Analysis Systems Make the Difference." *National Real Estate Investor*, May, 1986.

Harwood, Bruce. *Real Estate: An Introduction to the Profession*, 3rd ed., Reston, VA: Reston Publishing Company, 1983.

Mader, Chris, with Jon Bortz. *The Dow Jones-Irwin Guide to Real Estate Investing*, rev. ed., Homewood, IL: Dow Jones-Irwin, 1983.

Pyhrr, Stephen A., and James R. Cooper. *Real Estate Investment*. New York: John Wiley & Sons, Inc., 1982.

Reilly, John. W. *The Language of Real Estate*. 2nd ed. Chicago: Real Estate Education Company, 1982.

Richards, Robert William. *The Dow Jones-Irwin Dictionary of Financial Planning*. Homewood, IL: Dow Jones-Irwin, 1986.

Seldin, Maury, ed. *The Real Estate Handbook*. Homewood, IL: Dow Jones-Irwin, 1980.

Appendix B
B

GLOSSARY

ABSTRACT OF TITLE—Summary of all recorded documents and judgments in the history of a real estate title.

ACCELERATION CLAUSE—Statement inserted in a mortgage that gives the mortgagee the right to demand the balance due on a mortgage when a provision in the loan contract has been violated by the mortgagor (e.g., when title of property is transferred, as in selling).

ADVERSE POSSESSION—Method of acquiring title to real property by openly and notoriously occupying the property of another as the lawful owner over a continuous period of time as required by state law.

APPRAISAL—A means of estimating the fair market price of real estate using a market comparison or other approach.

AS IS—Property sold without guarantees, stated or implied, as to quantity, quality, or condition. Buyer becomes responsible for quantity, quality, and condition of property immediately after sale in the absence of fraud on the part of the seller.

BONA FIDE—1. In good faith. 2. Without intent to defraud.

CASH FLOW—Total cash received less total cash outlay (other than capitalized expenditures) in a real estate project.

CLOSING COSTS—Amounts paid for processing and finalizing the transfer of real estate, such as lender's fees, attorney's fees, surveys, title insurance, etc.

CLOUD ON TITLE—1. Defective title. 2. An encumbrance against the property that will prevent the transfer of a warranty deed until the cloud is removed (e.g., fraud in conveyance of title).

COMPARATIVE ANALYSIS—The simultaneous consideration of two or more prospective investments on comparable grounds.

CONDEMNATION—The procedures required in eminent domain to buy privately owned real estate from an unwilling owner for the good of the public; the owner must receive ''just compensation'' for the property.

CONTRACT—1. An agreement between two or more people. 2. For real estate purchases: a written agreement for valid consideration, offer and acceptance, legal capacity to contract, and subject matter must not violate public policy. The agreement must be signed by all parties.

DEED—1. Conveyance of title to real estate. 2. A legal document conveying title to real property. (See Warranty Deed and Quitclaim deed.)

DOWN PAYMENT—In a purchase transaction, money paid by the buyer which reduces the balance of the purchase price for purposes of establishing the amount borrowed. The down payment usually includes the earnest money deposit and is typically completed at closing.

DUE ON SALE CLAUSE—See Acceleration Clause.

EARNEST MONEY—An immediate deposit required to establish a bona fide offer to buy real estate which may be deducted from a selling price at closing (as part of a down payment) or may be returned if the sale contract is not completed. Generally, the greater the amount of earnest money deposited, the more motivated a buyer is.

EASEMENT—The right to use land, usually a strip, owned by another. Easements are used to provide access to property that is landlocked by another property and to the right of ways for utilities, railroads, highways, streets, sidewalks, alleyways, etc. Generally, easements become attached to the property and passed on as an encumbrance to the title when the property is sold.

ECONOMIC OBSOLESCENCE (Economic depreciation)—A decrease in the value of property because of factors outside the property and beyond the owner's control (i.e., a residential structure is devalued when a new commercial airport has landings and takeoffs nearby).

EMINENT DOMAIN—The authority of a government (federal, state, or local), and sometimes a public utility, to buy privately owned real estate from an unwilling seller through condemnation; and provides for the owner to receive fair market value for the property. (See Condemnation.)

ENCROACHMENT—An unauthorized intrusion of a structure or other fixture from one person's property onto the property of another.

ENCUMBRANCE—Any claim against the property (e.g., lien, mortgage, or easement). Encumbered property usually means attached liability. (See Cloud on Title.)

ESCHEAT—The property of an owner who dies intestate and without known lawful heirs is reverted to the state (i.e., the property *escheats* to the state).

FAIR MARKET VALUE—1. The estimated price of real estate made by appraisal. 2. An assumed price at which a willing buyer and willing seller will make a transaction when neither is unduly compelled to act and both parties possess relevant knowledge.

FEASIBILITY ANALYSIS—A financial summary of specified variables for the purpose of determining whether a prospective investment will fit within certain constraints.

FEE SIMPLE (Fee Absolute, Fee Simple Absolute, or Absolute)— The right of real estate owners to use and dispose of their real property as they choose, limited only by state and federal laws. Highest form of ownership: complete and unrestricted control.

FEE SIMPLE DEFEASIBLE—An estate in real estate that could subsequently be annulled or revoked under certain conditions (e.g., a deed contains the condition that a certain property can only be used for a public school building or the grantor will retain ownership). Such an estate cannot be revoked so long as the specifications are adhered to.

FSBO—For Sale By Owner (fiz-bo).

GRANTEE—The recipient of a property transfer, such as a purchaser.

GRANTOR—The transferor, such as a seller.

HOMESTEAD PROTECTION LAWS—Provided in some states to exclude the principal homestead of a debtor from forced sale; most states do not include the home mortgage under this protection.

JUDGMENT LIEN—Claim placed against the property of a debtor by a court of law after a claimant has shown just cause for the property to be held in security for a lawful debt.

LEVERAGE—Purchasing by borrowing part or all of the purchase price.

LIEN—A claim or encumbrance placed against property for the payment of a debt; it may be against a specific property or against all the property of the debtor. (See Mortgage Lien, Mechanic's Lien, Tax Lien, and Judgment Lien.)

LIQUIDATE—1. To convert to cash by selling equity. 2. To eliminate a debt (e.g., a mortgage by paying the full amount).

LIQUIDITY—1. Ability of property to command market value when converted into cash. 2. The ease with which a given property can be sold at or near market value.

MECHANIC'S LIEN—A claim placed against real estate for labor and materials used to build, maintain, or improve such property.

MORTGAGEE—The recipient of a mortgage (i.e., the lender).

MORTGAGOR—The provider of the mortgage (i.e., the borrower).

MORTGAGE LIEN—A claim placed against mortgaged property for

payment of the mortgage; typically, it is placed against the property at the time the mortgage is accepted by the lender.

NET OPERATING INCOME (NOI)—An amount equal to gross rental income less vacancy losses, credit losses, and operating expenses. It is used in computing cash flow after income taxes.

NONRECOURSE LOAN—A loan made to purchase property without causing the borrower to become personally liable for repayment. The property itself is the sole security for repayment.

PITI—Principal, Interest, Taxes, Insurance.

PRIVATE MORTGAGE INSURANCE (PMI)—Generally, insurance provided by private companies (rather than FHA or VA) and designed to cover a certain portion of a loan on real property, essentially for the sake of the lender, enabling such a lender to loan up to 95 percent the property value.

POINT—One percent of the amount of a loan. Generally, points, as opposed to closing costs, are required to obtain a below-market loan so that the lender's compensation will be comparable to the prevailing market yield. Normally, points may be paid by either buyer or seller as stated in a sales contract or purchase agreement.

PURCHASE AGREEMENT—A sales contract.

QUALIFIED FEE ESTATE—An estate in real property subject to limitations placed on the deed by a previous owner (e.g., a provision in a will where property ownership is transferred to a spouse so long as she does not remarry).

QUALIFYING A BUYER—1. By the lender: making an estimate of a prospective buyer's financial ability to pay for a specific property. 2. By broker or salesperson: an estimate of a buyer's desires, motivation, needs, emotions, and financial qualifications for purchasing real estate.

QUITCLAIM DEED—A deed that is transferred without any claim, warranty, or other rights of ownership by the seller; is often used to clear a cloud from a title, especially where the chain of ownership is broken by abandonment and the former owners cannot be contacted.

REAL ESTATE (Realty)—1. Land with all the buildings and structures attached thereto. 2. For investment purposes: land, buildings, and other fixtures considered as space in which the production of income is expected over a period of time.

REAL ESTATE BROKER—A person licensed and regulated by state government to act as an independent agent in real estate business.

REAL ESTATE MARKET—The demand for and availability of real estate in a given location.

REAL ESTATE SALESPERSON—A person licensed by a state board to arrange for the listing, selling, trading, renting, and leasing of real estate belonging to others in return for compensation as an agent of a real estate broker.

REVERSE LEVERAGE—Occurs when property is bought with a down payment and a loan and the property's value drops below the purchase price. In effect, the rate of loss for the out-of-pocket investment (down payment) will be greater than the rate of loss for the entire investment

RISK—The degree of unpredictability of an actual rate of return of a prospective investment. Also, the probability that an unavoidable or unexpected event will devalue the investment, thereby reducing or eliminating income.

SALES CONTRACT—An agreement between a buyer and a seller generally specifying all pertinent terms of a sale.

TAX LIEN—A claim against the property of an owner for failure to pay any kind of taxes—local, state, or federal.

"SUBJECT TO"—See Nonrecourse Loan.

WARRANTY DEED (General Warranty Deed)—A deed from the seller to the buyer which fully warrants that good clean title to the property is transferred. Warranty deeds are the most common and offer the best protection for a grantee.

ZONE—Area of restricted land use established by local government (e.g., an industrial park, or a single-family, detached-home residential area).

ZONING ORDINANCES—City or county laws that define real estate usage in a given area.

Appendix
C

SOFTWARE FOR INVESTORS
IN RESIDENTIAL PROPERTY

For IBM PC

REAL ESTATE FEASIBILITY ANALYSIS TEMPLATE
(Requires Lotus 123)

For investors in residential properties to be placed in service during 1987 and beyond, IRR with reinvestment rate and borrowing rate, after-tax cash flow projections, 10-year amortization schedule, debt-service one month in arrears, and month placed in service option ($45). (A less advanced version, which is included on the template, was used in preparing the cash flow analyses in this book.)

RE Templates
c/o Bert Richards
628 Pepperwood Lane
Stone Mountain, GA 30087
(404) 658-4468

EX-RE INVESTOR TEMPLATES
(Requires Lotus 123)

For records of equity, cash flow projections, taxes, after taxes, IRR, expenses, mortages, etc.

L B Associates
8817 Skokie Lane
Vienna, VA 22180
(703) 938-9093

HOME WORKS

For real estate salespersons, lawyers, home buyers, bankers, investors. Mortgage payments; amortization payments and schedules; case management; etc.

Keep It Simple Software, Inc.
211 East 43rd Street
New York, NY 10017
(800) 848-8909

REAL PROPERTY MANAGEMENT

In addition to management records and functions, makes detailed analysis of residential and commerical properties.

Real-Comp Inc.
P.O. Box 1263
Cupertino, CA 95015
(408) 996-1160

PROPERTY MANAGEMENT

For the management of residential and commercial properties; management records; operating statements; check writing and reconciliation; financial records, etc.

> Yardi Systems
> 3324 State Street, Suite "0"
> Santa Barbara, CA 93105
> (805) 687-4245

REAL ESTATE ANALYZER

For residential and commercial properties; analyzes property from relevant data and extrapolates current and potential profitability; is suited for analyzing financial alternatives, including the effects of taxes.

> HowardSoft
> 1224 Prospect Street, #150
> La Jolla, CA 92037
> (619) 454-0121

RESORT PROPERTY MANAGEMENT

For properties that rent on daily, weekly or monthly basis; automatic searching for available units; management records, check writing, monthly and annual owner statements, etc.

> Run-time Contemporary Computer Services, Inc.
> P.O. Box 3086
> Atlantic Beach, N.C. 28512-3086
> (919) 247-3130

PROPERTY MANAGEMENT

Specifically designed for commercial, single-family units, and HUD properties; handles rent receipts, delinquent payments, vacancies, vendors; writes checks and makes financial statements on each property, etc.

REAL ESTATE
(For the cassette driven computers, PC-1/PC-3)

Computes annuities, interests, depreciation, commissions, cash flow analysis, amortization, etc.

INVESTMENT ANALYSIS
(For the TRS III)

Designed for broker, investor, lender, or appraiser; computes developmental analysis, ROR, projections, etc.

All computer analyses vary with the requirements, expectations, and needs of individual users. Therefore, we cannot recommend any program, except the one we have used in preparing this book (Real Estate Feasibility Analysis Template), which requires Lotus 123, version 2.

Appendix
D

ABOUT THE AUTHORS

ROBERT W. RICHARDS is a lecturer in the School of Accountancy at Georgia State University. He is a CPA and earned his Master of Taxation degree from GSU in 1981. Mr. Richards is a real estate tax consultant, financial advisor, and a public speaker on real estate and tax topics. He is author of *The Financial Planner's Tax Almanac, The Dow-Jones Irwin Dictionary of Financial Planning,* and *Maximize Your Gains: Tax Strategies for Today's Investor.*

GROVER RICHARDS is a retired realtor associate, psychologist, professor of psychology and Lieutenant Colonel, U.S. Army. He has been an active real estate investor throughout the South-Eastern and South-Western United States. Since retiring four years ago, Mr. Richards has continued to invest in Georgia real estate, and has expanded his interest and knowledge in real estate investing.

Appendix
E

CHAPTER 3 PROBLEM SOLUTION

CASH FLOW ANALYSIS — RESIDENTIAL REAL ESTATE   ADDRESS:

** THIS INVESTMENT MEETS YOUR CRITERIA **

PURCHASE PRICE	$140,000	PERCENT ALLOCATED TO BUILDING	83%
ESTIMATED RATE OF VALUE INCREASE PER YEAR	7%	FUTURE VALUE	$171,506
EXPECTED YEARS OF OWNERSHIP	3	SELLING EXPENSES	5%
PERCENT OF PURCHASE PRICE TO BE FINANCED	90%	MARGINAL TAX BRACKET	28%
BORROWING RATE 10.00%		REQUIRED RATE OF RETURN ON INVESTMENT OUTLAY	25.00%
AMOUNT BORROWED $126,000		MONTH PLACED IN-SERVICE (JAN = 1)	1
PAYBACK PERIOD (YRS.) 30			
PAYMENT (MONTHLY) $1,106			
FAIR MONTHLY RENTAL	$1,200		
ESTIMATED INCREASE PER YEAR	3%		
VACANCIES AND CREDIT LOSSES	10%		
ANNUAL OPERATING EXPENSES	$1,500		
ESTIMATED INCREASE PER YEAR	10%		
DEPRECIATION (27.5 YEARS, STRAIGHT LINE)	3.64%		

	YEAR 1	2	3	4	5	6	7	8	9	10
GROSS RENTAL INCOME	$14,400	$14,832	$15,277	$15,735	$16,207	$16,694	$17,194	$17,710	$18,241	$18,789
VACANCIES & CREDIT LOSSES	(1,440)	(1,483)	(1,528)	(1,574)	(1,621)	(1,669)	(1,719)	(1,771)	(1,824)	(1,879)
OPERATING EXPENSES	(1,500)	(1,650)	(1,815)	(1,997)	(2,196)	(2,416)	(2,657)	(2,923)	(3,215)	(3,537)
NET OPERATING INCOME	$11,460	$11,699	$11,934	$12,165	$12,390	$12,608	$12,818	$13,016	$13,202	$13,373
INTEREST DEDUCTION	(12,568)	(12,495)	(12,414)	(12,325)	(12,226)	(12,116)	(11,996)	(11,863)	(11,715)	(11,553)
DEPRECIATION DEDUCTION	(4,066)	(4,242)	(4,066)	(4,242)	(4,242)	(4,242)	(4,242)	(4,242)	(4,242)	(4,242)
TAXABLE INCOME (LOSS)	($5,174)	($5,039)	($4,546)	($4,402)	($4,078)	($3,750)	($3,421)	($3,089)	($2,756)	($2,422)
NET OPERATING INCOME	$11,460	$11,699	$11,934	$12,165	$12,390	$12,608	$12,818	$13,016	$13,202	$13,373
DEBT SERVICE	(13,269)	(13,269)	(13,269)	(13,269)	(13,269)	(13,269)	(13,269)	(13,269)	(13,269)	(13,269)
CASH FLOW BEFORE TAXES	($1,809)	($1,570)	($1,335)	($1,104)	($878)	($660)	($451)	($253)	($67)	$104
TAX BENEFIT (PAYMENT)	1,449	1,411	1,273	1,233	1,142	1,050	958	865	772	678
NET CASH FLOW	($360)	($159)	($62)	$129	$263	$390	$506	$612	$705	$782
APPROX LOAN BAL @ YR END	$125,300	$124,526	$123,671	$122,727	$121,684	$120,731	$119,258	$117,852	$116,298	$114,582

SALES ANALYSIS - - - - - - - - - - - - -   PRESENT VALUE OF CASH FLOWS (@ REQUIRED RATE) - - - - - - - -

SALES ANALYSIS		PRESENT VALUE OF CASH FLOWS	
SELLING PRICE	$171,506	PRESENT VALUE OF NET CASH FLOW YR1	($288)
SELLING EXPENSES	(8,575)	PRESENT VALUE OF NET CASH FLOW YR2	(102)
MORTGAGE BALANCE	(123,671)	PRESENT VALUE OF NET CASH FLOW YR3	(32)
		PRESENT VALUE OF NET CASH FLOW YR4	0
PROCEEDS BEFORE TAXES	$39,260	PRESENT VALUE OF NET CASH FLOW YR5	0
ADDITIONAL TAX PAID	(9,885)	PRESENT VALUE OF NET CASH FLOW YR6	0
		PRESENT VALUE OF NET CASH FLOW YR7	0
NET SALES PROCEEDS	$29,374	PRESENT VALUE OF NET CASH FLOW YR8	0
		PRESENT VALUE OF NET CASH FLOW YR9	0
		PRESENT VALUE OF NET CASH FLOW YR10	0
		PRESENT VALUE OF NET SALES PROCEEDS	15,040
		TOTAL PV OF INVESTMENT @ REQUIRED RATE	$14,618
		TOTAL EQUITY INVESTMENT	(14,000)
		NET PRESENT VALUE	$618

CHAPTER 7 PROBLEM SOLUTION
ALTERNATIVE B

CASH FLOW ANALYSIS -- RESIDENTIAL REAL ESTATE   ADDRESS:

** THIS INVESTMENT DOES NOT MEET YOUR CRITERIA **

PURCHASE PRICE	$135,000	PERCENT ALLOCATED TO BUILDING	92%
ESTIMATED RATE OF VALUE INCREASE PER YEAR	6%	FUTURE VALUE	$170,434
EXPECTED YEARS OF OWNERSHIP	4	SELLING EXPENSES	3%
PERCENT OF PURCHASE PRICE TO BE FINANCED	0%	MARGINAL TAX BRACKET	28%
BORROWING RATE	8.70%	REQUIRED RATE OF RETURN ON INVESTMENT OUTLAY	12.00%
AMOUNT BORROWED	$0	MONTH PLACED IN SERVICE (JAN = 1)	1
PAYBACK PERIOD (YRS.)	30		
PAYMENT (MONTHLY)	$0		
FAIR MONTHLY RENTAL	$1,100		
ESTIMATED INCREASE PER YEAR	3%		
VACANCIES AND CREDIT LOSSES	10%		
ANNUAL OPERATING EXPENSES	$2,000		
ESTIMATED INCREASE PER YEAR	10%		
DEPRECIATION (27.5 YEARS, STRAIGHT LINE)	3.64%		

	YEAR 1	2	3	4	5	6	7	8	9	10
GROSS RENTAL INCOME	$13,200	$13,596	$14,004	$14,424	$14,857	$15,302	$15,761	$16,234	$16,721	$17,223
VACANCIES & CREDIT LOSSES	(1,320)	(1,360)	(1,400)	(1,442)	(1,486)	(1,530)	(1,576)	(1,623)	(1,672)	(1,722)
OPERATING EXPENSES	(2,000)	(2,200)	(2,420)	(2,662)	(2,928)	(3,221)	(3,543)	(3,897)	(4,287)	(4,716)
NET OPERATING INCOME	$9,880	$10,036	$10,183	$10,320	$10,443	$10,551	$10,642	$10,713	$10,762	$10,785
INTEREST DEDUCTION	0	0	0	0	0	0	0	0	0	0
DEPRECIATION DEDUCTION	(4,328)	(4,516)	(4,516)	(4,328)	(4,516)	(4,516)	(4,516)	(4,516)	(4,516)	(4,516)
TAXABLE INCOME (LOSS)	$5,552	$5,520	$5,667	$5,991	$5,926	$6,035	$6,126	$6,197	$6,246	$6,268
NET OPERATING INCOME	$9,880	$10,036	$10,183	$10,320	$10,443	$10,551	$10,642	$10,713	$10,762	$10,785
DEBT SERVICE	0	0	0	0	0	0	0	0	0	0
CASH FLOW BEFORE TAXES	$9,880	$10,036	$10,183	$10,320	$10,443	$10,551	$10,642	$10,713	$10,762	$10,785
TAX BENEFIT (PAYMENT)	(1,555)	(1,546)	(1,587)	(1,678)	(1,659)	(1,690)	(1,715)	(1,735)	(1,749)	(1,755)
NET CASH FLOW	$8,325	$8,491	$8,597	$8,642	$8,783	$8,861	$8,927	$8,978	$9,013	$9,030
APPROX LOAN BAL @ YR END	$0	$0	$0	$0	$0	$0	$0	$0	$0	$0

SALES ANALYSIS   - - - - - - - - - - - - -   PRESENT VALUE OF CASH FLOWS (@ REQUIRED RATE) - - - - - - - - -

SELLING PRICE	$170,434	PRESENT VALUE OF NET CASH FLOW YR1	$7,433	
SELLING EXPENSES	(5,113)	PRESENT VALUE OF NET CASH FLOW YR2	6,769	
MORTGAGE BALANCE	0	PRESENT VALUE OF NET CASH FLOW YR3	6,119	
		PRESENT VALUE OF NET CASH FLOW YR4	5,492	
PROCEEDS BEFORE TAXES	$165,321	PRESENT VALUE OF NET CASH FLOW YR5	0	
ADDITIONAL TAX PAID	(13,443)	PRESENT VALUE OF NET CASH FLOW YR6	0	
		PRESENT VALUE OF NET CASH FLOW YR7	0	
NET SALES PROCEEDS	$151,878	PRESENT VALUE OF NET CASH FLOW YR8	0	
		PRESENT VALUE OF NET CASH FLOW YR9	0	
		PRESENT VALUE OF NET CASH FLOW YR10	0	
		PRESENT VALUE OF NET SALES PROCEEDS	96,521	
		TOTAL PV OF INVESTMENT @ REQUIRED RATE	$122,335	
		TOTAL EQUITY INVESTMENT	(135,000)	
		NET PRESENT VALUE	($12,665)	

CHAPTER 7 PROBLEM SOLUTION
ALTERNATIVE C

CASH FLOW ANALYSIS — RESIDENTIAL REAL ESTATE   ADDRESS:

** THIS INVESTMENT MEETS YOUR CRITERIA **

PURCHASE PRICE	$135,000	PERCENT ALLOCATED TO BUILDING		92%
ESTIMATED RATE OF VALUE INCREASE PER YEAR	6%	FUTURE VALUE		$170,434
EXPECTED YEARS OF OWNERSHIP	4	SELLING EXPENSES		3%
PERCENT OF PURCHASE PRICE TO BE FINANCED	90%	MARGINAL TAX BRACKET		28%
BORROWING RATE	8.70%	REQUIRED RATE OF RETURN ON INVESTMENT OUTLAY		26.00%
AMOUNT BORROWED	$121,500	MONTH PLACED IN SERVICE (JAN = 1)		1
PAYBACK PERIOD (YRS.)	30			
PAYMENT (MONTHLY)	$952			
FAIR MONTHLY RENTAL	$1,100			
ESTIMATED INCREASE PER YEAR	3%			
VACANCIES AND CREDIT LOSSES	10%			
ANNUAL OPERATING EXPENSES	$2,000			
ESTIMATED INCREASE PER YEAR	10%			
DEPRECIATION (27.5 YEARS, STRAIGHT LINE)	3.64%			

	YEAR 1	2	3	4	5	6	7	8	9	10
GROSS RENTAL INCOME	$13,200	$13,596	$14,004	$14,424	$14,857	$15,302	$15,761	$16,234	$16,721	$17,223
VACANCIES & CREDIT LOSSES	(1,320)	(1,360)	(1,400)	(1,442)	(1,486)	(1,530)	(1,576)	(1,623)	(1,672)	(1,722)
OPERATING EXPENSES	(2,000)	(2,200)	(2,420)	(2,662)	(2,928)	(3,221)	(3,543)	(3,897)	(4,287)	(4,716)
NET OPERATING INCOME	$9,880	$10,036	$10,183	$10,320	$10,443	$10,551	$10,642	$10,713	$10,762	$10,785
INTEREST DEDUCTION	(10,536)	(10,456)	(10,369)	(10,274)	(10,170)	(10,057)	(9,934)	(9,800)	(9,653)	(9,493)
DEPRECIATION DEDUCTION	(4,328)	(4,516)	(4,516)	(4,328)	(4,516)	(4,516)	(4,516)	(4,516)	(4,516)	(4,516)
TAXABLE INCOME (LOSS)	($4,984)	($4,936)	($4,702)	($4,282)	($4,244)	($4,022)	($3,808)	($3,603)	($3,407)	($3,225)
NET OPERATING INCOME	$9,880	$10,036	$10,183	$10,320	$10,443	$10,551	$10,642	$10,713	$10,762	$10,785
DEBT SERVICE	(11,418)	(11,418)	(11,418)	(11,418)	(11,418)	(11,418)	(11,418)	(11,418)	(11,418)	(11,418)
CASH FLOW BEFORE TAXES	($1,538)	($1,382)	($1,235)	($1,098)	($975)	($867)	($776)	($705)	($656)	($633)
TAX BENEFIT (PAYMENT)	1,396	1,382	1,316	1,199	1,188	1,126	1,066	1,009	954	903
NET CASH FLOW	($143)	$0	$82	$101	$213	$259	$290	$304	$298	$270
APPROX LOAN BAL @ YR END	$120,618	$119,656	$118,607	$117,462	$116,215	$115,089	$113,370	$111,751	$109,986	$108,061

SALES ANALYSIS - - - - - - - - - - - -

PRESENT VALUE OF CASH FLOWS (@ REQUIRED RATE) - - - - - - - - -

SELLING PRICE	$170,434	PRESENT VALUE OF NET CASH FLOW YR1	($113)
SELLING EXPENSES	(5,113)	PRESENT VALUE OF NET CASH FLOW YR2	0
MORTGAGE BALANCE	(117,462)	PRESENT VALUE OF NET CASH FLOW YR3	41
		PRESENT VALUE OF NET CASH FLOW YR4	40
PROCEEDS BEFORE TAXES	$47,859	PRESENT VALUE OF NET CASH FLOW YR5	0
ADDITIONAL TAX PAID	(13,443)	PRESENT VALUE OF NET CASH FLOW YR6	0
		PRESENT VALUE OF NET CASH FLOW YR7	0
NET SALES PROCEEDS	$34,416	PRESENT VALUE OF NET CASH FLOW YR8	0
		PRESENT VALUE OF NET CASH FLOW YR9	0
		PRESENT VALUE OF NET CASH FLOW YR10	0
		PRESENT VALUE OF NET SALES PROCEEDS	13,655
		TOTAL PV OF INVESTMENT @ REQUIRED RATE	$13,623
		TOTAL EQUITY INVESTMENT	(13,500)
		NET PRESENT VALUE	$123